The American Exploration and Travel Series

CALIFORNIA IN 1792

California in 1792
A Spanish Naval Visit

by

Donald C. Cutter

UNIVERSITY OF OKLAHOMA PRESS : NORMAN AND LONDON

Written or Edited by Donald C. Cutter

The Discovery of Gold in California (Sacramento, 1950)

The Four Ages of Tsurai (coauthor) (Berkeley and Los Angeles, 1952)

The Diary of Ensign Gabriel Moraga's Expedition of Discovery in the Sacramento Valley, 1808 (Los Angeles, 1957)

Malaspina in California (San Francisco, 1960)

Over the Santa Fe Trail in 1857, by William B. Napton (ed.) (Santa Fe, 1964)

Tadeo Haenke v el final de una vieja polémica (coauthor) (Buenos Aires, 1966)

The California Coast: A Bilingual Edition of Documents from the Sutro Collection (Norman, 1969)

Journal of Tomás de Suría of His Voyage with Malaspina to the Northwest Coast of America in 1791 (ed.) (Fairfield, Wash., 1980)

California in 1792: A Spanish Naval Visit (Norman, 1990)

Library of Congress Cataloging-in-Publication Data
Cutter, Donald C.
    California in 1792 : a Spanish naval visit / by Donald C. Cutter.
    — 1st ed.
        p.   cm. — (The American exploration and travel series ; v. 71)
    Includes bibliographical references and index.
    ISBN 0-8061-2306-0 (alk. paper)
    1. California—Description and travel—To 1848.
    2. Spaniards—California—History—18th century.
    3. California—Discovery and exploration.   I. Title.   II. Series.
F864.C95   1990
979.4'02—dc20   90-50231
                                            CIP

California in 1792: A Spanish Naval Visit is Volume 71 in The American Exploration and Travel Series.

Contents

Illustrations   ix
Preface   xi
Part One. Editor's Introduction
1. Introduction   3
2. California in the Early 1790s   27
3. Dramatis Personae   49
4. Homeward to San Blas   95
Part Two. The Report: The Voyage of the Spanish
    Schooners *Sutil* and *Mexicana*, 1792   101
Bibliography   169
Index   173

Illustrations

Profiles of the Coasts of Modern-day Washington
and Oregon by José Cardero   *Page* 16
Map of the Port and Bay of Monterey, 1791   18
José Cardero's Copy of Juan de Pantoja's Map
of the Port of San Francisco, 1792   48
Cayetano Valdés   54
Dionisio Alcalá Galiano   60
Modo de Pelear de los Indios de Californias, by José Cardero   70
*Vista del Convento, Yglecia y Rancherías de la Misión
del Carmelo,* by José Cardero   83
José Cardero's Copy of the San Blas Pilots' Map   96
Profiles of the Coast near Cape Mendocino, the Farallones
de San Francisco, and the Fondeadero de Monterey,
by José Cardero   110
Tetra regio montanus, by José Cardero   115
Anonymous Bird of Monterey, by José Cardero   116
Gracula, by José Cardero   116
Picus, by José Cardero   117
Vista del Presidio de Monte Rey, by José Cardero   122
Plaza del Precidio de Monte Rey, Ascribed to José Cardero   123
Plaza del Precidio de Monte Rey, Ascribed to José Cardero   125
Soldado de Monterey, Ascribed to José Cardero   126
Mujer de un soldado de Monterey, Ascribed to José Cardero   127

Misión del Carmelo de Monterey, Ascribed to José Cardero 130–31
India y Indio de Monterey, by José Cardero 135
Indio de Monterey, Ascribed to José Cardero 136
"Status of the Missions of New California . . . 1791"
(*Estado de las Misiones de la Nueva California . . . 1791*) 159
"Status of the Missions of New California in the Years
Indicated" (*Estado de las Misiones de la nueva
California en los años que se expresa*), 1792 160

Preface

Columbus discovered America in 1492 in command of three tiny vessels sailing westward from Palos de Moguer near the mouth of Spain's Rio Tinto. Three hundred years later, Dionisio Alcalá Galiano and Cayetano Valdés completed the job of exploration that Columbus had advanced appreciably in his day. The 1792 voyage of the Spanish schooners *Sutil* and *Mexicana* mapped the last section of unexplored Pacific coastline during a summer of constant hydrographic activity. It was an outstanding feat of seamanship in vessels so small that Columbus's flagship, the *Santa María,* was about equal to the combined tonnage of the two 1792 schooners. Columbus's *Niña,* his smallest vessel, was about the same tonnage as either the *Sutil* or the *Mexicana.*

Three centuries are a long time to complete a task that today appears easy. But the Pacific Northwest Coast of the continent of North America was long neglected, being one of the parts of the globe leftover from the era of early exploration. Both Spanish concern and international interest finally coincided there in the last half of the eighteenth century.

With discovery of the Pacific Ocean by Vasco Núñez de Balboa in 1513, followed shortly by Fernando Magellan's epic crossing of that huge expanse of water, Spain laid claim to a substantial fraction of the world. Núñez de Balboa's act of possession, as magnificent as it was preposterous, strengthened by papal sanction and by a treaty with Portugal, formed the basis for Spain's claim to exclusive sovereignty over the great Pacific Ocean as well as to the scattered islands contained therein. With very little contrary effective interest by other European powers, for over two hundred years Spain's expansive claim was rarely contested, and even when challenged, such interludes were of brief duration.

Spanish presence in the Pacific included its sixteenth century conquest of the Philippine Islands, and of a later way station at Guam in the Marianas. A regular trade route from Acapulco in Mexico to Manila evolved with the latter city as Spain's foothold in the Orient, through which were funneled valuable trade goods, both outbound and inbound. Aboard overloaded, poorly defended, and cumbersome galleons, the treasures of two worlds crossed the Pacific for well over two centuries.

Despite crossings on an annual basis, and sometimes more frequently, Spain failed to unlock many of the secrets of exotic Oceania. This was owing to satisfaction with existing sailing directions, from which there was little variation, as well as to national reluctance to publicize such discoveries as were made from time to time.

Spain's splendid isolation was finally disturbed by news of Russian explorations out of Siberia toward Alaska and by published reports of British Captain James Cook's voyages. Spurred into action, Spain vigorously played out a losing hand. A series of bold steps set the stage for the last search for the frequently sought strait through North America that had eluded European seekers. First, in 1769, under the leadership of Visitor General José de Gálvez in Mexico, Spain determined to extend its colonial frontier hundreds of miles northward by occupation of the Upper California ports of San Diego and Monterey. A supporting move was establishment of a naval base and shipbuilding facility at the unpleasant location of San Blas on the coast of Nayarit, Mexico. Ships from that home port were used not only to support the new colonization effort but also to explore the coast some 1,500 additional miles northward to Alaskan waters.

To legitimize Spanish claim, acts of possession were frequent along the coast. Attention was given to map making and to keeping detailed journals of exploration. As a final step, Spain established two posts in northern latitudes: one at Nootka Sound in 1789 and a second of brief duration at Núñez Gaona at Neah Bay in what is today the state of Washington.

The flowering of Spanish interest in the Pacific Northwest coincided with the inception and implementation of Spain's great naval exploratory contribution to the Enlightenment. That was the five-year-long cruise of the corvettes *Descubierta* and *Atrevida,* an expedition organized to emulate and possibly to surpass the achievements of Captain Cook. The enterprise was entrusted to Captains Alejandro Malaspina and José Bustamante of the Spanish Navy, with the former playing the greater role. Initially there had been no intention of Malaspina's group paying a visit to northern latitudes. Rather, the corvettes were originally tasked to visit the Hawaiian Islands en route from Mexico to the Philippines.

An international incident at Nootka Sound, involving seizure of British merchant ships and imprisonment of their sailors by the commanding officer of a Spanish naval vessel, resulted in a change of plans for the naval scientific exploring expedition. Among the new objectives was that of making a last and thorough search for the strait leading through North America from the Pacific to the Atlantic. A second was to visit the tenuous settlement at Nootka and report on its status and viability. The more pleasant prospect of a Hawaiian sojourn was canceled.

One summer, that of 1791, was insufficient time to complete the assigned tasks, though much progress was made. It was as a follow-up to the 1791 effort that in the summer of 1792 the newly constructed schooners *Sutil* and *Mexicana,* products of the San Blas shipyard, were sent to finish what the larger vessels had not fully accomplished. With great diligence, and by dint of continuous effort, the small schooners did what was needed.

Both the Malaspina group in 1791 and *Sutil* and *Mexicana* in 1792 made a brief stay at Monterey, capital of California. On both occasions recuperation was the primary motive for such a stop on the way south back to Mexico. Both groups made reports on the little-known colony of Upper California, but these reports were not for immediate release. Malaspina's comments became part of his larger account, while the manuscript journal of the voyage of the *Sutil* and *Mexicana* was soon in demand because it contained material appropriate to the diplomatic negotiations resulting from the Nootka Sound Controversy, as the diplomatic problem with Great Britain has been called.

In considerable measure, the details of Malaspina's 1791 visit to California are already published.[1] The present work focuses on the operations of the *Sutil* and *Mexicana* from the Strait of Juan de Fuca to their home port of San Blas, and particularly on the month-long stay in Monterey. The work depicts conditions in California in the 1790s, provides biographical information concerning the visitors and the visited, and concludes with an annotated translation of the most-complete extant journal.

Concerning the 1792 visit to California, there has been little written, and even this has been based on a greatly reduced version of what had been recorded at that time. Ten years after those events, in 1802, an anonymous, though official, two-volume work was published in Madrid bearing the title *Relación del viage hecho por las goletas Sutil y Mexicana en el año de 1792*. Volume 1 had an exceedingly long introduction concerning Spanish naval activity in the Pacific, but little concerning the *Relación*. The second volume was a slim atlas containing copper-plate engravings of drawings and maps associated in various degrees with the 1791 or 1792 explorations, though not always directly.

An English language edition including a translation of the 1802 *Relación* was published in London in 1930 by Lionel Cecil Jane as *A Spanish Voyage to Vancouver and the Northwest Coast of America*. The great bibliophile Henry Raup Wagner treated the expedition extensively in his *Spanish Explorations in the Strait of Juan de Fuca*

[1] Donald C. Cutter, *Malaspina in California* (San Francisco, 1960).

(Santa Ana, Calif., 1933). In 1958, José Porrúa Turanzas reprinted the 1802 edition without change in his Colección Chimalistac series. In 1971, AMS Press in New York reprinted the earlier English version, ascribing thereto the editorial intervention of José Espinosa y Tello, a common error. In none of these publications was there any attempt to reconstruct the original journal.

The most complete version of the 1792 account was written with occasional footnotes, which in the present edition are set apart by quotation marks, and attributed to the "JOURNAL," to identify them as part of the original account. My additions to such notes are appended in square brackets. All notes, whether from the journal or editorial additions, are numbered serially.

Permission to publish in translation Manuscript 1060, "Vargas Ponce," of the Naval Museum of Madrid was granted by its director, Capitán de Navío José María de Zumalacárregui. Additional help with aspects of the present study was frequently given by María Luisa Martín-Merás and Dolores Higueras, both of whom serve in the position of *jefe de investigación* of the Museo Naval and have for many years been involved with study of different aspects of the Malaspina expedition.

DONALD C. CUTTER
Albuquerque, New Mexico

PART ONE

1. Introduction

In late September 1792 two small vessels manned by tired crews sighted the prominent headland of Cape Mendocino in northern California. The schooners were headed southward along the Pacific Coast in accordance with orders, only partially followed, to inspect the littoral from the Strait of Juan de Fuca to Monterey. Built hastily in Mexico with an eye to close-order exploration, the two 46-ton vessels, *Nuestra Señora del Carmen* and *María Santísima de la Asunción,* had long since forgotten their official names and sailed out of their home port of San Blas as the *Sutil* and the *Mexicana.* In command were two youthful Spanish naval officers, Commanders Dionisio Alcalá Galiano and Cayetano Valdés.

During the summer of 1792 the small task force had explored and prepared data and rough sketches for a map of the labyrinth of waterways around Vancouver Island on the Northwest Coast. The explorers had first gone to Nootka, locale of Spain's precarious northern outpost of Santa Cruz de Nutka. There they made final preparations for intensive survey activity. The *Sutil* and *Mexicana* entered the target area via the Strait of Juan de Fuca and finally exited through Goletas Channel, returning to Nootka. In so doing, they became the first vessels to circumnavigate fully the Pacific Coast's largest island. It had been a hard summer's work with much time spent at the oars of their rowboats.

California, already known to many of those aboard, was an inviting prospect where the young officers would have ample space

3

to draw the final charts resulting from their observations, and where the crews could enjoy the pleasant surroundings. But what had motivated all of this little-known Spanish activity?

In September of the previous year, 1791, the most ambitious of Spain's scientific exploratory endeavors, the expedition commanded by Captains Alejandro Malaspina and José Bustamante, had placed California for a fortnight under the intensive scrutiny by an elite corps of investigators. That visit, like the subsequent stay of the schooners *Sutil* and *Mexicana,* had in considerable measure been a rest-and-recuperation stop for the Malaspina group after a summer dedicated to a fruitless search for the Northwest Passage and to an inquiry into the logic of a continued Spanish physical presence in the Pacific Northwest.

Malaspina's twin exploratory vessels, the much-larger corvettes *Descubierta* and *Atrevida,* had sailed down the coast from a northing of about 60°. Malaspina had done much to dispel the myth of a practicable passage between the Atlantic and Pacific oceans. He had also investigated Spain's modest foothold at Nootka Sound, where a two-year-old colony stood as an expensive token garrison. After Malaspina's 1791 Pacific Northwest campaign, which was a small fraction of his extended voyage, there remained only one unexplored and still-possible area that might contain the important geopolitical waterway known as the Strait of Anian or the Strait of Ferrer Maldonado, or by whatever other name the desired Northwest Passage might be called. The neglected area was the maze of islands, inlets, and straits extending south of Nootka and then inland and around Vancouver Island. Access to this area was via the broad waterway already named for the ancient mariner Juan de Fuca, reportedly a Greek. His story, probably fictitious, forms part of the Spanish version of the legend of the northern strait. Pressing duties elsewhere had prevented Malaspina from entering the strait in 1791, but by the time he had returned to Acapulco, including his brief September stay in Monterey, Malaspina had determined that his group would have to make a follow-up reconnaissance in 1792 to finish what had been left undone. It was in response to this need that the schooners *Sutil* and *Mexicana* were sent to northern waters.

This important project of exploration of the inland waters behind Vancouver Island had been on Spanish Viceroy Revilla Gigedo's mind. He had already ordered construction of three small vessels, one of which he planned to use precisely for that purpose. His plan had called for sending north a sortie commanded by a very experienced young officer, Francisco Antonio Mourelle, a man in whom the viceroy had great confidence. Mourelle had extensive sailing experience and had been along the Northwest Coast as early as 1775 as second-in-command of the *Sonora*. Additional sea duty out of the Naval Department of San Blas added to his knowledge. Furthermore, just before this time Mourelle had been involved in gathering and editing documents concerning the northern discoveries of the Spanish Navy, and in many ways he was well prepared for such an exploratory assignment. However, Malaspina was eager to send some of his own men to carry out the unfinished task of the last search for the Strait of Anian.[1] He insisted that Alcalá Galiano and Valdés be sent and that two small, almost identical[2] vessels be sent rather than a single one as earlier planned.

Malaspina's desires were more easily made possible by an illness, a fever, that overcame Mourelle, which made the requested substitutions logical. The explorers professed regrets that there was little room and no available aid for anyone who might be ill, with the result that Mourelle was left behind amidst expressions of sorrow in not having the benefit of his company and knowledge.[3]

Having disposed of Mourelle, it was even easier to ring in artist José Cardero as a substitute for the previously assigned second

[1] Revilla Gigedo to Lerena, México, November 30, 1791, in Archivo General de Indias (AGI), Audiencia de México 1545.

[2] John Kendrick, "The Brig *Sutil*—Its Hull, Rig and Equipment," MS report, 1987, courtesy of the author, who indicates that the hull designs of the two vessels were identical, but that they carried different rigging. The *Sutil* was a brig and the *Mexicana* a topsail schooner.

[3] Cayetano Valdés to Revilla Gigedo, Acapulco, February 8, 1792, in Archivo General de la Nación (AGN), Marina 82.

pilot, Juan Carrasco, who like Mourelle already had considerable experience along the coast. In a letter to the viceroy, Cayetano Valdés pointed out that, though Carrasco had brought the two exploratory schooners to Acapulco from the shipyard at San Blas where they had been constructed, he did not have the desired capacity as an artist, "having no other skills than those of a normal pilot," and therefore would be of no great utility, but rather would be in the way because of the scarcity of quarters.[4] Malaspina also detached ten other members of the crew of the *Descubierta* who went as volunteers to help man the two exploratory vessels.[5] The resulting combined initial complement of the two vessels was thirty-nine.[6]

Though at no place in the documentation concerning the complement of the *Sutil* and *Mexicana* is there evidence of a close personal friendship, the feeling emerges that Cayetano Valdés and Dionisio Alcalá Galiano were more than incidental shipmates and coparticipants in the Malaspina expedition. Their assignment to northern waters in 1792 seems to have strengthened their previous bond of professional comradery. Both were from Andalusia, both were from families of substance, and both were eminently successful in their naval careers up to that point. From the extant documentation, many letters of which were jointly signed by the two young captains, there is reinforcement of an idea of personal closeness.

Just as the two commanders were joined by mutual experience, background, and nautical interests, one has a strong feeling that either or both men had a professional and perhaps personal interest in the young artist-cartographer-scribe-pilot, José Cardero, who also was an Andalusian. It is clear that both Alcalá Galiano and Valdés were pleased to have his participation, perhaps having

[4] Alcalá Galiano to Revilla Gigedo, Acapulco, February 14, 1792, in AGN, Marina 82, and C. Valdés to Revilla Gigedo, Acapulco, February 8, 1792, in AGN, Marina 82.

[5] Pedro de Novo y Colson, ed., *Viaje político-científico alrededor del mundo por las corbetas Descubierta y Atrevida . . .* (Madrid, 1885), pp. 205–6.

[6] Details of the complement of the *Sutil* and *Mexicana* are in an *estado* of March 8, 1792, in AGN, Marina 82.

suggested to Malaspina the detachment of Cardero from the main exploratory group. Such an assignment not only was potentially useful to the newly named captains of the *Sutil* and *Mexicana,* but also saved Cardero from regressing to a position of potential oblivion. In Malaspina's instructions [7] Cardero was to continue to receive the paltry salary of twenty pesos a month, which is what he had been assigned "when he was with the corvettes [*Descubierta* and *Atrevida*] when he was a beginner at drawing and worked very few hours." [8] Since his new assignment was for full-time work, as well as full responsibility for the maps of the forthcoming expedition, and since Carrasco's salary would have been seventy pesos even if he were not capable of so much work, the two captains suggested an eighty-peso-per-month figure to the viceroy. Revilla Gigedo countered with a sixty-peso offer, plus some possible later adjustments. [9]

By the time the small schooners were made ready and the season of the year was appropriate for operations in northern waters, the Malaspina vessels were several steps along their five-year itinerary, exploring in the Philippine Islands. Therefore the small, two-schooner task force was on its own without higher-command guidance. Overall command rested with Alcalá Galiano on the *Sutil.* He was thirty years old with fourteen years of prior service to his credit. Command of the *Mexicana* fell to Cayetano Valdés, who was five years Alcalá Galiano's junior, though both had the same date of rank as commanders in the Spanish Navy. Secundino Salamanca was the other commissioned officer on the *Sutil,* and Juan Vernacci served in a similar position on the *Mexicana.* All four officers are mentioned with some frequency in the account of the voyage.

The fifth identifiable major participant in the expedition, the one-time cabin boy and later the official artist, José ("Pepe") Car-

---

[7] Malaspina's instructions for the *Sutil* and *Mexicana* are found in Archivo Histórico Nacional (AHN), Estado 4288. They are dated December 14, 1791, at Acapulco.

[8] Concerning Cardero's salary, Alcalá Galiano and C. Valdés wrote to Revilla Gigedo on March 3, 1792, in AGN, Marina 82.

[9] Alcalá Galiano and C. Valdés to Revilla Gigedo, México, March 17, 1793, in AGN, Marina 82.

dero, was never mentioned, even though he was a major contributor to the pictorial records of both the Malaspina expedition and the voyage of the *Sutil* and *Mexicana*. Since he sailed aboard the latter under Valdés, it is possible that Cardero had enlisted originally in 1789 to serve as an orderly to that officer. His artistic talent became a pleasant bonus for Malaspina. Though untrained in art, Cardero drew frequently and painstakingly, and already had achieved some success before he was detached to serve on the *Mexicana*. Aboard that schooner, the diminutive, twenty-five-year-old Andalusian from Ecija not only was the artist but also acted as scribe, pilot, mapmaker, and possibly journalist.

Cardero played a varied role. The existing drawings done by him in 1792 while aboard the *Mexicana* are a treasury of early Pacific Northwest Coast art.[10] Besides drawing, he frequently wrote letters on his own behalf, never showing any reluctance to rate his participation as anything short of essential. He also penned letters for other prominent persons, not only his commanders but also figures associated with the Naval Department of San Blas. His bold, stylized handwriting, appropriate for a person of artistic talent, is easily recognized among the archival documents. It almost jumps from the pages to greet the researcher.

Strangely, Cardero is never mentioned by name in the 1792 journal. This seems possible only if he were its author, especially in view of the frequent references to the four commissioned officers. Letters exist written by the commanders attesting to the importance of Cardero's participation in the voyage, which are hardly in accord with the silence concerning the artist in the pages of the journal.[11] This lack of mention has led a modern scholar to assume that Cardero did not even accompany the schooners in 1792.

Cardero was an original member of the Malaspina expedition, though in a humble capacity. His life as an artist began with his work at Guayaquil, Ecuador. When a shortage of capable artists

[10] Most of the known drawings by José Cardero are reproduced in Carmen Sotos Serrano, *Los Pintores de la expedición de Alejandro Malaspina*, 2 vols. (Madrid, 1982).
[11] Alcalá Galiano and C. Valdés to Revilla Gigedo, México, March 3, 1793, in AGN, Marina 82.

developed, the explorers had gladly accepted the young man's services. With time his efforts improved, and though he was never officially an artist with the main Malaspina group, he did have the distinction of being so named in association with the *Sutil* and *Mexicana*. The appointment also brought an elevation in both pay and status.

The most complete version of the 1792 account of the voyage of the schooners—the one translated here concerning the visit of those vessels to California early in the fall of 1792—is in the clear handwriting of the artist Cardero. Concerning California, the earliest draft is almost four times as long as the version that was later accepted for publication in 1802. The contents of this original manuscript lend new insight into the formative years of the province. Particular emphasis was placed on the missions, and especially on the figure of their gentlemanly Father President Fermín Francisco de Lasuén. There is an extended portion concerning the role of the presidio, and particularly on the part played by presidial soldiers in the operation of the colony. Some of the material dealing with Indians is based on Father Miguel Venegas's early comments on Baja California natives, a considerable portion of which is inappropriate to a precise evaluation of the native cultures being observed firsthand in 1792.

It is difficult to determine, even when faced with certain documentary statements concerning responsibility for the journal, who actually wrote it and under what circumstances. Was Cardero's role that of principal author, or just that of a scribe taking dictation? A question arises when authority is attributed to Alcalá Galiano. Was he the "author" merely because he was the senior commander and therefore responsible for the final report as a chain-of-command function? Furthermore, the draft that seems to be the closest to the original is in the hand of José Cardero, who was on the *Mexicana* while Alcalá Galiano commanded the *Sutil*. When the ships were in port, it would have been quite possible for Cardero to act as scribe for the overall commander, but for comments of activity while under way, it hardly seems probable.

Complicating identification of the true author is the fact that the long "original draft" has many corrections, alterations, and deletions. These were done principally by someone other than Cardero. Most of the corrections are in the hand of Alcalá Galiano, leaving one with the impression that, if he was the original author, he also served as his own very critical editor, for many of the changes are stylistic, and almost none are substantive. Most changes seem to be more the sort of thing that some editors do for lack of anything else to do—change for the sake of change rather than for clarity or for felicity of expression. Some additional corrections, made by Malaspina, are almost all very minor. It is hard initially to determine the circumstances of such corrections as are clearly in the tight penmanship of Malaspina. These would have had to be done not only after completion of the operations of the *Sutil* and *Mexicana* in 1792 but also after the completion, in September 1794, of the much-longer voyage of the *Descubierta* and *Atrevida,* since Malaspina had no earlier contact with the schooners nor with their officers.

Certain factors support the argument in favor of Cardero as the true author. That he might have had more time aboard vessels that were undermanned, under-officered, and undersized, favors him as author. It may also just qualify him as a good scribe. That he frequently acted as amanuensis is a point against Cardero's authorship. Whatever the truth may be, it is the "earliest" version, that in Cardero's handwriting, before editorial tightening at times made that version nearly unrecognizable, that is here presented in translation.

The manuscript in Cardero's hand is located today in the Museo Naval of the Spanish Ministry of the Navy in Madrid. It is archival manuscript number 1060 and forms part of a bound volume including some "corrected" copies of accounts of the same voyage.[12] The outside title of the bound volume is "Vargas Ponce," a name associated with the Spanish Navy at that time, but in no way connected with the Malaspina expedition. José Vargas Ponce in his

[12] A similar document, but incomplete as regards overall length, is found in Viaje al Estrecho de Fuca, tomo 2, ff. 41–54, MS 144 in Museo Naval (MN).

involvement with the hydrographic depository, predecessor of the Museo Naval, may have been responsible for accessioning the manuscript under consideration. Manuscript 1060 has a break of a single folio. Fortunately that missing sheet was found in a manuscript volume entitled Miscelánea, manuscript 2420 of the Museo Naval. The single folio bears no relationship to the other documents contained in Miscelánea 2420 and is clearly out of place archivally in that volume, which was recently organized and formally accessioned in the Museo Naval, and which consists of precisely what the title indicates—miscellany. Separated from the main document probably because of the statistics involved, the fugitive folio contains on one side the California mission statistics of 1785, 1790, and 1791. The verso side has a continuation of the 1792 journal comments.

Turning to the document itself, we see that the text is at times identical to what Malaspina intended to publish at a later time. This could be because Malaspina's final report relied partly on information gathered in 1792 rather than entirely on what had been gathered in 1791. Furthermore, four of the five principal participants were making a second visit to California, and they were recalling their earlier observations. The exception was the senior commander, Alcalá Galiano, who in 1791 had remained in Mexico engaged on other objectives of the Malaspina expedition. It would have been strange had there not been a general consensus among observations made only a year apart. A second visit had the benefit of augmenting the total body of information, and there was no reason to keep the two visits separate in the report.

For reasons treated later, Malaspina's principal findings went unpublished for nearly a century, whereas the 1792 account, greatly reduced in length, was first printed in 1802, making the former seem more a copy of the latter than vice versa. At neither time was there nearly as much material printed as is contained in manuscript 1060, which gives us much fresh information about a period concerning which there has been notable recent interest. Examples of this interest are the publication of Father Francis F.

Guest's excellent biography of Father Fermín Francisco de Lasuén [13] and the writings of that same California prelate translated and edited by Father Finbar Kenneally. [14] This 1792 report treats aspects of that Franciscan's leadership that have hitherto been unavailable. Particularly interesting are Lasuén's attempts to deal with the native languages at San Carlos Mission in order to produce a catechism for religious instruction. Though Lasuén has already been appreciated by historians for his merits, and though he was the subject of repeated favorable comments by visitors La Pérouse, Malaspina, and Vancouver, the 1792 visit augments their accounts with additional details of Lasuén's priestly ministry and timely help. His substantial vocabulary list and the catechism in Rumsen and Esselen are unique contributions. [15]

Much as the journal writer appreciated the spirit of Franciscan activity in California, he also indicates how that missionary effort could have been more successful if priests had been given greater preparation at the home College of San Fernando in Mexico City before setting out for the mission field. Insufficient linguistic training, lack of understanding of native psychology, and a need for greater and more timely support from the agents of the crown are pointed out as problem areas.

Criticism is leveled at the neglect by government of the local presidial soldiers, who are painted in colors more glowing than logic would suggest. One can find motives not only because the visitors were service personnel, but also because the military had been most cordial and helpful in both 1791 and 1792 in support of the explorers' aims. Added to those was a true concern for the lot of frontier soldiers. It would have been hard to have received a more laudatory assessment than was given, and this in absence on both occasions of the governor, who was also the senior military commander of New California. The partiality for the enlisted person-

---

[13] Francis F. Guest, *Fermín Francisco de Lasuén (1736–1803): A Biography* (Washington, D.C., 1973).

[14] Finbar Kenneally, trans. and ed., *The Writings of Fermín Francisco de Lasuén*, 2 vols. (Washington, D.C., 1965).

[15] Reproduced below in the translation of the journal.

nel, without mention of the officers, may argue for the author also being an enlisted man—José Cardero.

The journalist gave the local Indians very little credit for basic intelligence. His lengthy negative assessment is double-barreled, since the personal investigations and observations were corroborated by earlier Jesuit evaluations of California Indians much farther south. Modern anthropologists are quick to defend local California Indian culture, but the Rumsen and Esselen Indians rated very low when judged by contemporary Spanish standards, even among the natural scientists with Malaspina, who were greatly interested in native cultures in their far-ranging studies. The Rumsen and Esselen Indians may have suffered unduly from comparison with the recently visited native groups of the Pacific Northwest Coast.

Some of the descriptions penned by the 1792 journalist are visually enhanced in the pictorial archive that emanated from the entire Malaspina expedition. Although it is thought that the artwork done at Monterey in September 1791 was by both Tomás de Suria and José Cardero, there exists a possibility that Cardero may have done some of his drawings in 1792, since he spent over twice as much time in California on the second occasion. In either case, some items depicted are verbally reinforced in the report of the second visit. Examples are the double enclosure of the presidio, the nearby corral, the dress of the local Indians, the native huts on the slope outside the mission compound at San Carlos, and other minor details.

The substantial 1792 report adds to the existing bibliography of early visitors' accounts and to what they said about the early period of California occupation. The Count of La Pérouse, George Vancouver, Georg von Langsdorff, and other noteworthy visitors left us glimpses of the past, and we are endebted to them. As outsiders they saw things with alien eyes. Each visitor picked up details that escaped inclusion in military reports, in mission documentation, and in administrative records. Each visiting group had special points of view. La Pérouse compared the missions to the slave plantations of Santo Domingo. Vancouver was dubious of the ability of the California military to mount even a token defense in case of attack, and Langsdorff pointed out the economic debility of a province without trade. Unlike the aforementioned foreigners, the visitors of 1791 and 1792 were Spanish nationals who could appreciate the successes and evaluate the failures of their fellow countrymen.

For the 1792 party California was a secondary stop. The primary mission of the visitors had already been accomplished. They had beaten the odds that had favored a disaster overtaking their undersized ships.[16] They had completed the planned circumnavigation of the big island off which lay the Spanish post at Nootka Sound. Originally their exploration had been intended as a cooperative effort with Captain George Vancouver of the British Royal Navy, but the *Sutil* and *Mexicana* operated mostly independently in their trip counterclockwise around what was soon to be called Vancouver Island.

Secondary instructions called for a closer inspection of the entire Pacific Coast from Nootka south to San Blas, a long coastline passed frequently by Spanish vessels and already recipient of many Spanish place-names, but not as yet mapped with great confidence, particularly the Washington-Oregon coast. When the explorers were en route south out of Nootka, three days of east winds drove the tiny schooners well out to sea. It cost them three more days to recover a position suitable for the coastal reconnaissance stipulated in the viceregal orders. On September 7, 1792, at dawn during a period of clearing weather, the mariners sighted the Washington coast at 47°, slightly north of the undetected entrance to Grays Harbor. From their position they spied in the distance the snowcaps of the Cascade Range, and to the southeast a high mountain with a flat top that was far beyond the low-lying coast. The prominent mountain was certainly Mount Saint Helens, as it appeared before the great eruption of 1980 changed its silhouette.

A reappearance of fog, the warning noise of the nearby surf, and the shallowness of the ocean determined a change of course, head-

[16] Journal entry, in Vargas Ponce, MS1060, MN, f. 66.

ing more southward than east. By noon, before visibility was greatly reduced by heavy fog, Cape Shoalwater was sighted. As evening approached, José Cardero found opportunity to do the first of three views of the coast as seen from aboard. It is dated most precisely of any artistic effort of the Spanish on the Northwest Coast—7:00 P.M., September 7, 1792—and is given the title "View of the Coast and of a Mountain of whitish earth bearing NNE." There is a mistake in Cardero's bearing: the direction probably was meant to be "SSE." The configuration of the prominent whitish geographical feature is that of Saddle Mountain (3,300 feet), and on the far right is Neahkahnie Mountain, with Tillamook Head in the foreground.

The next two of Cardero's coastal views, assuming orderly progression along the coast, must have been done on September 8. His "View of the Coast north of Hezeta Entrance, with the highest mountain bearing 140° at a distance of 8 leagues from the coast and snow-covered down to its foothills," has Cape Disappointment in the foreground. Both the distance and direction of the "highest mountain," probably Mount Saint Helens, are way off. Thirty-five leagues and a bearing of 72° are more accurate. The latter direction is identical with that attributed to the final view and perhaps a transposition was made in the final copy.

The third view is from farther south and bears the descriptive legend "View of Hezeta Entrance or Columbia River, with the highest mountain bearing 72° at a distance of 9 leagues from the coast. From a distance its north point seems to be an island." Recognizable here are two features of Cape Disappointment, specifically North Head (which seems to be an island) and McKenzie's Head, an appropriately bald spot near the end of the cape. The "highest mountain" should continue to be Saint Helens. The direction would be accurate, and the distance, though obviously far off, would logically be one league greater than in the second view.[17]

[17] Geographical determinations presented here have been greatly aided by Herbert K. Beals, of the Oregon Historical Society, who provided me with maps, photographs, and his interpretations. I have agreed with most of his hypotheses, including the idea that Mount Saint Helens would have presented an apparent multiple-peak

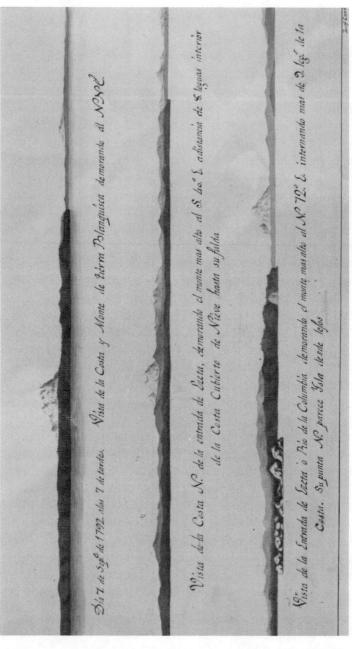

Profiles of the coasts of the modern-day states of Washington and Oregon by José Cardeno, September 7, 1792 (*Vista de la Costa . . . , Vista . . . de la Entrada de Ezeta, Vista de la Entrada de Ezeta o Río de la Columbia*). Museo Naval, Madrid.

Frequent contrary weather foiled much of the effort to follow closely the coast from the mouth of the Columbia River south to Monterey, though in 1791 there had been greater success, as is evident from Cardero's coastal profiles done a year earlier. In 1792 better results were obtained after leaving Monterey, as the *Sutil* and *Mexicana* were able to explore the Channel Islands and to rectify the position of those offshore islands, all of which had been poorly represented on the chart used by the Naval Department of San Blas, a copy of which the 1792 explorers had with them.[18]

Curiously, at the very time that Alcalá Galiano and Valdés were busily engaged in placing the final touches on their map that completed the outline of the Pacific Coast, the date of the tricentennial of the Columbian discovery of America came and went, apparently unnoticed. In light of the modern yearly celebration of Columbus Day, or Día de la Raza, as a national holiday in Spain, and of the international importance given to the quadricentennial of that event, and particularly if one bears in mind the preparation for celebration of the five-hundredth anniversary, it seems natural that an appropriate acknowledgment of the tricentennial might have been held in California with Spanish mariners, local officers and residents, and Franciscan missionaries gathered for such purpose. Nor is it easily argued that facilities for such commemoration were lacking. Father Lasuén, in a letter of October 20, 1792, wrote to the father guardian of his college in Mexico City indicating that the *Sutil* and *Mexicana* had arrived on September 23, that he had paid them a visit on the twenty-fourth, and that on the twenty-fifth the explorers had attended Mass, "and all who travelled in the cabin of both vessels, and of the Frigate *Gertrudis,* dined at the mission. There were twenty-one of us at table. I am enclosing copies of the letter that I sent to the captains of those schooners regarding a gift they made me, and of their answer."[19]

---

configuration if Mount Adams and Mount Saint Helens were nearly lined up, which seems to have been the case.

[18] The San Blas pilots' map is reproduced on p. 96.

[19] Lasuén to Father Guardian [Tomás Pangua], San Carlos Mission, October 20, 1792, in Kenneally, *Writings of Lasuén* 1 : 256–58.

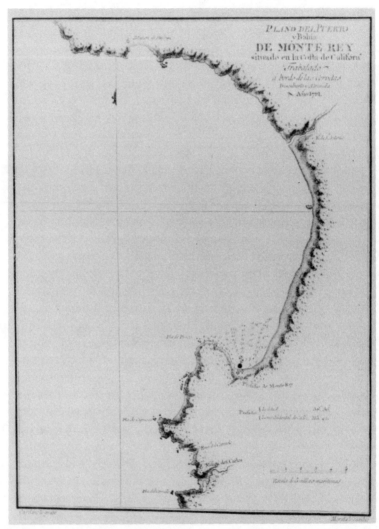

Map of the port and bay of Monterey, 1791. In *Relación del viage hecho por las goletas Sutil y Mexicana en al año de 1792*, vol. 2, *Atlas para el viaje de las goletas Sutil y Mexicana* (Madrid, 1802).

By October 9, just three days before Columbus Day, Juan Francisco de la Bodega y Quadra, commandant of San Blas and Spanish commissioner in the Nootka settlement negotiations, had arrived in port. On October 10, Lasuén visited Bodega, and on the eleventh, "Quadra and many officers of all the vessels were here at the Mission for dinner." No commemoration was mentioned, and in the absence of a reference to it, one can conclude that the tricentennial did not concern the group greatly, if at all.

The map being done by Alcalá Galiano and Valdés, soon to be forwarded by fast mail to Mexico City, sounded the death knell to the long-cherished hope and illusive concept of a practicable transcontinental strait stretching from one ocean to the other. Three hundred years earlier European thought had been directed to the Orient, but the land mass of America had blocked the path. The greatly desired passage through it was never going to become a practical reality. The puzzling riddle of the early years of Spanish exploration, that of finding a way through, had at long last been negatively solved.

The 1792 visit to California was not vital to its primary mission. As a result, that portion of the account became greatly abridged in the later publication, certainly more so than the portions dealing with circumnavigation of Vancouver Island.

Following the Monterey stopover, upon his return to Mexico, Alcalá Galiano received a letter from the Viceroy Conde de Revilla Gigedo acknowledging receipt of the maps and an extract of the journal. With his congratulations, the viceroy returned the journal and an errata sheet with copious criticism of spelling, grammar, and even some facts, for "corrections."[20] After those changes were made, and after spending some time in Mexico, the important members of the 1792 exploring expedition all finally returned to Spain, but not together, and to several different destinations. Reportedly, Juan Vernacci was involved in making some of the

[20] Viceroy Revilla Gigedo to Alcalá Galiano acknowledging receipt of *informe* and extract in AGN, Marina 92.

required corrections and was charged with final delivery of the amended manuscript.[21]

Meanwhile, the parent Malaspina expedition finally concluded its 62-month cruise and returned to Cádiz, whence it had sailed in June 1789. After a fruitful trip, rivaling those of the more famous Captain Cook, Malaspina came home to a hero's welcome, with appropriate promotion to commodore, and amidst plans to publish the results of his extended cruise. But the adulation abruptly turned sour when Malaspina became enmeshed in court intrigue and involved in political matters, the upshot of which was his arrest, trial, and imprisonment. It was prohibited even to mention his name in any publication based on the results of the naval scientific exploring expedition to which he had dedicated so much effort. He became a persona non grata, sent to prison for eight years, and finally was exiled to his native duchy of Parma, where he died, forgotten, in 1810 at Pontremoli. It was not until seventy-five years after his death that publication of Malaspina's labors was finally brought about by Pedro Novo y Colson, as *Viaje político-científico alrededor del mundo por las corbetas Descubierta y Atrevida, al mando de los capitanes de navío Don Alejandro Malaspina y Don José Bustamante y Guerra desde 1789 a 1794* (Madrid, 1885).

This publication was facilitated because, in the interval between his return to Spain and his trial, Malaspina had been busily engaged in placing in order for publication much of the material generated by his expedition. As indicated earlier, he obviously worked on the manuscript that Cardero penned concerning the 1792 voyage, making on it a few minor corrections. But when the manuscript was accepted for publication, Malaspina was in jail at La Coruña, and no mention was made of him by name in the edition that belatedly appeared in 1802.

Normally it might be expected that publications would clarify the authorship of the journal once and for all. Such was not the case, and the question remains, Just who did write it? There seem to be only five possibilities, the four commissioned officers and the

---

[21]Vernacci to A. Valdés, Cádiz, April 4, 1794, in Miscelánea, doc. 20, MS 2110 in MN.

artist Cardero. Although in the portion of the account dealing with the return trip from Nootka to San Blas, including the 33-day stopover at Monterey, there is scant specific mention of either of the seconds-in-command, there can be no doubt about their active participation at all times. But it is highly improbable that either Juan Vernacci or Secundino Salamanca were authors of the account that survives. That reduces the possibilities to three, the two captains and the artist-scribe. The least likely as author is the historically most prominent of the three, Cayetano Valdés. He lived until 1835, served as *capitán general* of the navy, was frequently decorated, and achieved high status both professionally and politically, yet there is never anything said about him as being author of the account of the voyage of the *Sutil* and *Mexicana*. Since he is mentioned often in terms of his participation as commander of one of the schooners, it would have been easy to lay claim to authorship if such were true. Also working against his authorship is the lack of any known published work written by him on any subject, despite a long public career.

The case for Dionisio Alcalá Galiano as author has greater merit. His untimely death in the Battle of Trafalgar in October 1805 made it impossible that he could in his later years harken back to his earlier literary accomplishment of writing the account. Writing was not out of character for Alcalá Galiano. In the period just after his association with the Malaspina enterprise, he was author of two works directly connected with his chief specializations of navigation and astronomy. In 1795 he wrote a brief *Memoria sobre el cálculo de la latitud del lugar por dos alturas de sol,* published in Madrid. The following year he authored *Memoria sobre las observaciones de latitud y longitud en el mar,* likewise published in Madrid. In neither of these works was there any mention that he was in the process of publication of the account of the 1792 voyage.

The case for Cardero has its strengths and weaknesses. As a frequent petitioner for both bureaucratic and royal favors, Cardero at no time stated that he wrote the account. The closest to any such recognition was his appointment as *contador de navío* (the equivalent of senior-grade lieutenant in the Naval Supply Corps), which was based on his good performance and work on the 1792 expedition of the *Sutil* and *Mexicana*.[22] In this royal appointment nothing was said about it being a reward for earlier activity from 1789 to 1791 with the main Malaspina expedition. Was such a spectacular promotion the result of drawing, acting as secretary, and serving as pilot? Or was it because he had performed unusually meritorious service as a jack-of-all trades, including authorship of the basic journal? Certainly the promotion from servant to naval lieutenant needs some logical explanation.

That the account has been referred to as Alcalá Galiano's journal may convince researchers that the youthful commander was the author. It may only mean that it was the journal of the expedition of which Alcalá Galiano was the senior officer.

Although Malaspina-expedition veteran and fellow officer José Espinosa was not present in 1792, the account has often been erroneously ascribed to him as either author or editor. Library listings and several publications have so credited Espinosa. This error is easily explained. The first edition of the account of the voyage of the *Sutil* and *Mexicana* was published in two volumes in 1802 as *Relación del viage hecho por las goletas Sutil y Mexicana en el año de 1792 para reconocer el estrecho de Fuca; con una introducción en que se da noticia de las expediciones executadas anteriormente por los españoles en busca del paso noroeste de la América.* Bound into the Museo Naval copy of the Relación was a report on astronomy signed by Espinosa, early director of the Depósito Hidrográfico, forerunner of the Museo Naval.

The intrusive twenty-page report bore the lengthy title "Memoria sobre las observaciones astronómicas, que han servido de fundamento a las Cartas de la costa NO de América, publicadas por la Dirección de trabajos hidrográficas, a continuación del viage de las goletas Sutil y Mexicana al estrecho de Juan de Fuca," and it was signed from Madrid on December 21, 1805, by Josef de Espinosa.

[22] Nombramiento del Contador de Navio de la Real Armada para d. Josef Cardero, Aranjuez, May 29, 1795, in Archivo-Museo Don Alvaro de Bazán, El Viso del Marqués (AMAB), Cuerpo de Ministerio, Asuntos Personales, José Cardero.

Without careful inspection of the contents of the work, his name, appearing as it did on the last page of a bound volume, conveyed the unintentional impression that Espinosa was responsible for the whole volume. Though the publishers in 1802 probably had the correct information available, there is no place in the book where Alcalá Galiano or Cardero or anyone else is indicated as author. The obvious result of such an erroneous ascription to Espinosa was that the true writer was no longer of any great concern, since bibliographic authority, even if incorrect, was established beyond any additional need.

If any person should be credited for editing the 1802 published account it is Martín Fernández de Navarrete, the famous Spanish naval historian. But he failed even to affix his name to the 167 pages of introduction to the *Relación*. Navarrete's introduction has almost nothing to say about the voyage of 1792 and a great deal to say about earlier Spanish naval activity.

If the saying that one picture is worth a thousand words is true, then José Cardero had a great deal to say about California even if it cannot be conclusively established that he was author of the original account of the visit, for his artistic production is of significant historical importance. Though the argument over the paternity of the account is inconclusive at this point and may never become any clearer, it can be summarized by saying that the most complete basic account is in Cardero's easily identified handwriting and that at no place is there acknowledgment of an author.

A longer version of the account of the voyage, but with much suppressed concerning California, was turned over to Viceroy Revilla Gigedo. The manuscript version, which was read attentively by that official partly because of poor penmanship and frequent defects in spelling, was in the hand of the senior officer, Alcalá Galiano. When that officer tried to defend himself in writing to the viceroy, he neither admitted having been author of the account, nor did he try to shift the blame to someone else. He admitted that the manuscript had not been sufficiently proofread because he had been ill and because he and his small group were making haste to return to Spain. The viceroy did not accept these as sufficiently valid excuses, indicating that had Alcalá Galiano asked for the services of a scribe, the viceroy would have supplied one and thus a good job would have been assured.

Besides the other defects, Revilla Gigedo pointed out that some of the place-names had been left off the maps submitted, specifically Points Moreno and de la Vega, the Island of Bonilla, Pacheco Channel, Points San Rafael and Langara, Wintuisen Entrance, Guemez Island, and Guemez Channel. The final two oversights are significant when one bears in mind that Guemez was one of the surnames of the viceroy. It would have been hard for him not to notice such a defect. [23]

The errata sheet provided by the viceroy listed seventy items that needed appropriate changes, some of which involved only the poor choice of a word or words. [24] If Alcalá Galiano were the author, these errors would reflect poorly on the level of his education. On the other hand, if such errors were introduced by a scribe who wrote the final copy, we would only blame Alcalá Galiano for inadequate proofreading. For whatever reason, proofreading does not seem to have concerned him greatly, but his role as a copy editor, however, neither establishes nor eliminates him as the original author.

Revilla Gigedo returned the manuscript "Relación" to Alcalá Galiano for corrections, some of which seem to have been made on the copy that is today manuscript 619 in the Museo Naval. Several widely scattered archives have copies of the errata list compiled by the viceroy, or by his subordinates; more errata sheets are found in the archives than there are copies of the "Relación" itself. [25] A series of letters exchanged in late 1792 and early 1793 between the viceroy and Alcalá Galiano [26] never clearly establishes just who

---

[23] Revilla Gigedo to Alcalá Galiano, México, October 23, 1793, in AHN, Estado 4290.

[24] Ibid. Also in Malaspina Correspondencia, tomo 3, MS 280, in MN.

[25] For example, in AGN, Marina 82 and 92, and in AHN, Estado 4290 (two copies).

[26] Malaspina, Correspondencia, tomo 3, MS 280, in MN.

wrote the account, though it is evident that as senior commander of the detachment it was Alcalá Galiano who bore the ultimate responsibility for the abbreviated existing report, and he was trying to minimize the importance of the errors that had been noted. On the other hand, the viceroy was pointing out the importance of having the manuscript in as good a shape as possible so that it might compare favorably with others that probably would soon be published.

Oddly, there is no mention of Cardero at any place in the official "Relación," nor of the artistic efforts that he had carried out with regularity on the Northwest Coast. This is hard to understand. He was later elevated to the rank of a commissioned officer on the basis of his contributions to the voyage of the *Sutil* and *Mexicana* to the Strait of Juan de Fuca, and with the enthusiastic recommendation of his commanders. It would seem that his name would have been mentioned on regular occasions, or at the very least on some occasion. Had Alcalá Galiano wanted to do so, it would have been easy to shift the blame to the former cabin boy whose name appeared nowhere.

At the time when the viceroy's suggestions had been incorporated into a revised manuscript, the prominent members of the party were no longer a unit. Valdés, Salamanca, and Cardero went from Mexico City to Veracruz in April 1793, took the *Minerva* to Havana, and from that Cuban port sailed to Spain on the *Cazador*. The three arrived in Cádiz in mid-June. Salamanca had been sent ahead to the court with such accounts as were not already in the possession of the royal authorities there. Cardero stayed behind in Cádiz with Valdés, who was ill but expected to follow shortly.

Meanwhile in America, Juan Vernacci was occupied for some time in hydrographic and cartographic efforts in Central America on the slight chance that there was a strait to be found through Nicaragua in Middle America. By October 1793, Vernacci and his commanding officer, Alcalá Galiano, were reunited, and they sailed together as officers aboard the war vessel *San Pedro de Alcántara*, headed for Havana. There Alcalá Galiano either volunteered or was ordered into service as commanding officer of the warship

San Juan Bautista. He served under Chief of Squadron Bernardo Muñoz in hostilities against the French in Santo Domingo and the Bahama Channel. Finally he returned to Spain, having been assigned as second-in-command of the warship *San Isidro,* aboard which he returned to Cádiz on October 26, 1794.[27]

Vernacci apparently remained aboard the *San Pedro de Alcántara* and arrived in Cádiz on April 2, 1794. He so notified the naval ministry two days later.[28] Though he carried "the original papers" of the voyage to the Pacific Northwest Coast, nothing is said about his being custodian of the artwork done in 1792 by Cardero, nor was there any identification concerning the author of the "Relación."

[27] The outline of Vernacci's return to Spain is reconstructed from various sources and is subject to possible future correction.

[28] Vernacci to A. Valdés, Cádiz, April 4, 1794, in Miscelánea, doc. 20, MS 2110, in MN.

2. California in the Early 1790s

Upper California had ceased to be the farthest outpost of Spanish colonial North America only three years before the visit of the *Sutil* and *Mexicana*. In 1789 that precarious position had been taken by the newly established military post at Santa Cruz de Nutka on Vancouver Island's west coast.[1] The existence of a much more remote colony than California made life in the older settlements more secure in that the previously tenuous lifeline of the Spanish Naval Department of San Blas was strengthened. Supply, a factor of great concern during California's minority, was now quite well assured. Instead of an occasional vessel from San Blas on the distant coast of Nayarit, by the 1790s there was much greater regularity of naval visits. This was a comfort, particularly insofar as there were frequent receipts of letters, packages, church ornaments, and supplies.

In another sense, these more frequent visits taxed the resources of California, since some vessels came there to obtain supplies for the northern garrison rather than go back to Mexico for such provisions. Such a resupply of naval stores and victuals was a mixed blessing as far as California was concerned. It provided an outlet for the surplus commodities that the young colony was capable of producing, for which local producers, whether at the missions or at

---

[1] An informal northern limit to Alta California, that used by the naval scientists, was 43° north latitude, or about sixty miles north of the modern boundary between the states of Oregon and California.

the towns, obtained payment either in money or, more often, on the books of the Spanish government. At the same time, such trade occasionally deprived locals of items that they needed only slightly less than the visiting mariners. Requests for supplies were seldom routine, but rather urgent in nature. It was only with considerable planning and soul-searching that the father president of the missions, which were not far above the subsistence level, could justify reducing stores at the missions in favor of meeting the urgent needs of the naval vessels. The problem was more acute in the off-season than in the time of maximum production. In brief, the Franciscans found themselves in the uncomfortable position of being responsible both to the government that had assigned them to California and to the Indian wards who had been entrusted to them by that same government.

California in the 1790s lacked population, as can be seen from the several statistical reports gathered by the visitors. Surprisingly, the most populous urban area was at the newest of the four presidios, Santa Barbara, with 230 inhabitants, followed in turn by San Diego, with 212, the capital city of Monterey, with 202, and San Francisco, with 144. The towns were even smaller, with Los Angeles, the most recently established, having the greater population, 131; and the northern town of San José de Guadalupe containing a mere 78. One demographic novelty in the reports was the listing of both Indian men and Indian women as "residents" at the presidios and in the towns.[2] A total of seventy-six Indians were thus included, indicating that detribalization and acculturation were taking place outside the missions. In the towns and at the presidios it may be assumed that much of the old native culture was rapidly discarded and new adjustments were being made to an altered environment. The cultural influence of the presidio was well presented by Max Moorhead in his book *The Presidio: Bastion of the Spanish Borderlands* (Norman, 1975). By extension, it is clear that the town was also a setting for unstructured Hispanicization of

[2] Compiled by Governor Pedro Fages and dated May 10, 1791, at Monterey. A translation is found in Cutter, *Malaspina in California,* opposite p. 82.

Native Americans who for some reason had not been incorporated into the pervasive mission system.

The expansion of missionary activity in California in the late eighteenth century is reflected in the statistics of the Franciscan establishments. Under the renowned Father Junípero Serra, nine missions were founded between 1769 and his death in 1784. These were located between San Diego de Alcalá on the south and San Francisco de Assisi on the north. Franciscan plans called for gradual filling in the intervening spaces with new missions. Two of these links in the larger chain were in the embryonic stage in 1791 and 1792. One was Santa Cruz, on the banks of the Rio San Lorenzo, directly north across open Monterey Bay from the capital and twenty-two miles distant. The second was Nuestra Señora de la Soledad, also near Monterey, about thirty-five miles up the Salinas River from its mouth. To establish these two new missions, Father Lasuén, Serra's successor as father president, had to scramble about to find the necessary ecclesiastical furnishings, while awaiting more appropriate ones which were slow in arriving from Mexico City. Early plans for setting up these missions had not reached fruition by 1790, but in 1791 efforts culminated in the official founding of Santa Cruz and La Soledad on August 28 and October 9, respectively.[3]

Since the founding period of the two new missions coincided with Malaspina's visit, Lasuén had requested that the naval expedition's commander lend needed assistance in the form of one of the corvette's boats to carry certain items from Monterey to the site of Santa Cruz. Despite his profuse praise for the Franciscan mission efforts and his extremely polite correspondence with the father president, Malaspina did not cooperate in the extension of mission activity. The naval leader apparently was more dedicated to the theory of Catholic evangelism than to its physical implementation. He was still in port when a packtrain left the capital with supplies for the new Santa Cruz mission.[4]

[3] A contemporary document signed by Lasuén gives April 28 as the founding date for Santa Cruz.

[4] Cutter, *Malaspina in California*, p. 50.

In contrast, though admittedly the circumstances were different, British Captain George Vancouver, as a visitor to California, made a substantial contribution to mission progress by some gifts, one-third of which were given to the new mission at La Soledad. These appreciated presents included nails, saws, axes, shovels, files, eating utensils, and an assortment of other items. Vancouver's gifts were reciprocated by Lasuén's presents of sixty abalone shells (items of prime importance in the maritime fur trade), six sheep, six sea-otter skins, and many sacks of vegetables, including potatoes.[5] Except for the cordial diplomacy involved, it would be easy to construe this reciprocal gift giving between the father president and the British commissioner in the Nootka Affair as a commercial exchange of goods, something forbidden by Spanish mercantilistic regulations.

On September 25, 1791, the actual day of Malaspina's departure from the anchorage at Monterey, Mission Santa Cruz was officially founded. Lasuén was not present, and the interim governor was represented by Ensign Hermenegildo Sal as his proxy. However, two weeks later the new mission at La Soledad was founded with both Father Lasuén and Acting Governor Argüello present. The second ceremony had been delayed by concern about helping the round-the-world explorers in their final preparations for departure.

In the 1790s the major hope for economic development of California lay in the mission system. During the colonial era the Hispanic population was never great in the province. Two early towns had been founded—San José in 1777 and Los Angeles in 1781. Colonial population never reached significant levels in the towns. Other Hispanic residents were the soldiers, who, with their families, lived within a presidial district with headquarters at one of the four military forts. Some families lived as military dependents near the actual presidios, or even within the walls of these forts; others accompanied their spouses or fathers on detached duty as part of the mission guard, the *escolta*. These mission support groups consisted of a corporal and six to eight soldiers. A few

[5] Kenneally, *Writings of Lasuén* 1 : 322.

additional military families, sometimes headed by a retired soldier, lived in the aforementioned towns.

Important in impact but not in numbers, and responsible in great measure for both the transfer and the preservation of Spanish culture, was the clerical component of society. All local priests were members of the Franciscan College of San Fernando headquartered in Mexico City. Most had been born in Spain. These Fernandinos ministered to the native California Indians who were attracted to the thirteen missions, including recently founded Santa Cruz and La Soledad. The missionaries were by their vows mendicants. They acted in loco parentis in dealing with the native converts, who were, by Spanish legal norms, the owners of the large mission estates that had been set aside by the crown and were under development. The total missionary population was approximately double the number of missions, since two priests were assigned to each mission. In addition, there was the father president and a few supernumerary priests. San Carlos Borromeo Mission, on the banks of the Rio Carmelo, was generally the headquarters for the father president because of its proximity to the capital at Monterey. The visits of 1791 and 1792 afforded the Spanish naval scientists the opportunity to see a well-organized mission in operation at San Carlos and to learn of the benevolent paternalism of the missions from the father president, clearly the most informed of all possible sources.

A final Hispanic element in the population of the province was the few rancheros, who with their families were engaged largely in livestock production. By 1792 there were very few Hispanic families who had been given land for such use. Rancho concessions of larger or smaller parcels of land are associated with a later period in California history. In fact, of the oft-mentioned Spanish land grants, almost all had their origins in the Mexican period. Those given at an early date were dispensed by the governor with a much less lavish hand than those of later date.

As for economic productivity, California was still in a most elementary stage in 1792. The missions produced only slightly more than their subsistence requirements. In theory, the towns were encouraged and even required to sell their surplus, if any, to the military. A list of set prices was promulgated in 1788 by Governor Fages.[6] Because of its interest, Malaspina's investigators obtained a copy of the price list which was later incorporated into the final Malaspina report concerning California.

A repeated concern of the visiting Spanish naval scientists was the economic health of Spain's overseas possessions. To determine this, Malaspina's men had made inquiries while in California and had carried out archival investigations in Mexico City in support of their field research. At Monterey they obtained statistical information in the form of a "General summary showing the advantageous condition in which the new establishments in northern California are found, and listing the presidios, missions, and towns of which it is comprised, the number of its inhabitants of both sexes, including children, the number of head of livestock they possess, and the *fanegas* of grain that they have recently harvested, and in a note the other things concerned with a thorough knowledge of its condition up until the end of 1790."[7] The summary was clearly the work of the recently retired, popular governor, Pedro Fages, and was dated at the Royal Presidio of Monterey on May 20, 1791. It had not been done by Malaspina's request, but it contained useful information on various aspects of provincial life. Mission statistics are regularly found in archival holdings, and Fages had these available to him. In addition, his summary contains town and presidial statistics, including rarer information on the livestock population at each of the three Royal Treasury stock farms that supported the military presence.

In a nonstatistical summary of conditions in California, Fages provided useful information concerning the early 1790s.

The towns are developing with obvious increase and are benefiting from the fertility of their lands, the abundance of water, and the other good qualities; and they guarantee the achievement of the

[6] Fages's price list of January 2, 1788, was still in effect. It is translated in Cutter, *Malaspina in California,* pp. 80–82.

[7] The summary, dated May 20, 1788, is translated in Cutter, *Malaspina in California,* pp. 82–83.

important ends for which they were founded. Both there and at the missions the crops have been good, and the extensive planting that has recently been completed is in generally good condition, meaning that it will be an abundant year.

Livestock increase to the utmost, to the extent that after the inhabitants eat all necessary for subsistence, there are so many that measures must be taken to prevent their dispersion, for there is no other outlet to maintain a satisfactory balance. Otherwise the gentiles will be given opportunity to kill them furtively, making it necessary to use force to correct this. The new governor [Roméu] is informed on this matter, so that he and all others concerned might carry out the rules upon which this depends, so that there be no change in the noted peace which is enjoyed. Concerning the notable lack of mules, this is already remedied by the breeding that the undersigned has succeeded in carrying out. Finally, the entire peninsula remains in a happy and peaceful state, with no exceptions to this worthy condition except the natives of the old missions who are affected to the maximum by syphilis.[8]

The visiting *Sutil* and *Mexicana* party, on their own account and independent of the earlier Malaspina inquiry, added an important document including mission economic statistics, which appears here in the translation of their report. This was a one-page summary of the "Status of the Missions of New California in the Years Indicated," which were 1785, 1790, and 1791. The document, which was provided by Father President Lasuén, concerns the first eleven missions. For the year 1790 it is similar but not identical to the figures in Governor Fages's "General Summary." One advantage of the "Status of the Missions" report is the comparisons that it offers of the years indicated. Also, because later mission summary reports are in the same form, it has a second advantage. The 1790 figures give ready access to a half decade of growth when compared with the 1785 enumeration, while the comparison of 1790 and 1791 depicts the growth of a single year, that between the visits of Malaspina and of Alcalá Galiano and Valdés. As regards the gathering of new data, this statistical report was one of the fresh contributions resulting from the 1792 visit, for it recorded final statistics on

[8] Cutter, *Malaspina in California*, p. 83.

the crop returns of 1791, which were incomplete for Malaspina in September 1791. Information contained therein demonstrates that after just over two decades California's mission wheat production yielded 17:1 for a total of 15,377 fanegas, or nearly 25,000 bushels. Barley yielded 24:1, for nearly 3,000 fanegas, while returns for maize, a much higher-yield grain, were 97:1, for a total of 7,625 fanegas. The as-yet-unharvested corn crop of 1792 yielded a high of 111:1, for 11,853 fanegas, the closest that corn ever came to equaling wheat production.

The early 1790s were a bonanza period for livestock production at the missions, conditioning the naval explorers' sanguine view of California stock-raising potential. Cattle had increased 65 percent in 1790, 29 percent in 1791, and 19 percent in 1792, when the census indicated over 30,000 head of mission cattle. To those were added over 5,000 head at the government stock farms operated by the presidios of Monterey, San Diego, and San Francisco, with another 2,400 head at the two towns, San José and Los Angeles.

Mission horse raising demonstrated similar patterns of growth of 56 percent, 18 percent, and 25 percent for those three years, with a total equine population of just under 4,000. The mission herds were outnumbered by the combined presidial (2,490) and town (1,500) livestock holdings. Mules were presidio-oriented animals, because of their importance to packtrains and mail delivery, and were most numerous at the forts. Unlike other frontier provinces, California had almost no burros.

Except for about 1,000 sheep owned by the *vecinos* (citizens) of the towns, the remaining animals in that category were in mission flocks. These were enjoying similar spectacular increases, from 21,415 in 1790 (a 67 percent increase since 1785) to 26,286 in 1791 (a 22 percent increase) and 31,906 in 1792 (a 21 percent increase). Goat and pig raising were comparatively unsubstantial.[9] In a separate report of December 1791[10] acquired by the members

[9] The general summary is in Cutter, *Malaspina in California*, facing p. 82. General economic production is treated in Robert Archibald, *The Economic Aspects of the California Missions* (Washington, D.C., 1978).
[10] Lasuén, Estado de las Misiones de la Nueva California sacado de los Informes de

of the *Sutil* and *Mexicana* contingent the total number of pigs at all the missions was 392. Goats totaled 4,040, with about half that figure in the combined herds of Missions San Juan Capistrano and San Gabriel. The 1792 visitors commented favorably on the governor's garden. This was a private garden developed by Pedro Fages beginning in 1783. It was located nearly a mile and a half from the Monterey Presidio and consisted of six hundred fruit trees, as well as shrubs and grapevines. On learning that his old companion in arms of the Sonora campaigns, José Antonio Roméu, was going to succeed him in office, Fages gave his garden to the new governor, saying in a letter, "You will find . . . nearby a garden which I have made at my own expense, from which you will have fine vegetables all the year, and will enjoy the fruits of the trees which I have planted." [11]

The visitors in both 1791 and 1792 soon were aware that California lacked effective leadership. Pedro Fages, a long-term administrator who served two nonconsecutive terms as senior military commander and civil governor, had sought retirement based on his advanced age, his years of service, and his wife's cherished desire to return to Mexico. Fages's petition for reassignment had been recently granted, and his departure in 1791 left the province in the hands of an acting governor who was serving when the Malaspina expedition made its visit in September 1791. Acting Governor José Dario Argüello was most cordial, attentive, and helpful to the naval exploratory group. Speculatively, it might be assumed that Fages would have been even more so. Such a supposition is based on the lavish and open friendship Fages and his wife had shown to the Count of La Pérouse when that French scientific explorer had visited Monterey in 1786. In 1791, Fages was a newly appointed colonel and would have had more resources and been of equivalent rank to Malaspina and Bustamante. Fages's long experi-

---

sus Ministros en fin de Diciembre del año 1791 in California y Costa N.O., vol. 1, MS 330, in MN.

[11] Fages to Roméu, quoted in Hubert H. Bancroft, *History of California* vol. 1 (San Francisco, 1884–90), pp. 482, 484.

ence since California's early beginnings would have been a great source of oral and possibly even documentary history.

By the time of Malaspina's arrival Fages had already left Monterey and was in southern California on the threshold of his final departure. The fruits of retirement slipped away from Fages when he died in late 1794, not long after his return to Mexico City, where he had been serving as an officer "without assignment," a euphemism for retirement.

Fages's replacement had already been determined prior to his departure. The new governor was José Antonio Roméu, a Valencian of appropriate experience. His background promised good things for the coastal province. Arriving with his wife, his family, and his adjutant, Sergeant Juan José Pérez Hernández, Roméu assumed his post as chief administrative officer and military commander in October 1791, just a few weeks after the corvettes *Descubierta* and *Atrevida* had sailed south from Monterey.

There is no clear picture of Roméu's brief period as governor. He suffered from ill health and was frequently sick both en route and after his arrival in California. Having received the last rites of the church, the short-term governor died in the arms of Franciscan Father President Lasuén at 10:00 A.M. on April 9, 1792.[12] The few records that exist concerning his governorship suggest local satisfaction and optimism concerning the future of the province under his guidance. Unlike Fages's well-planned departure from the California scene, Roméu's sudden death left the viceregal bureaucracy unprepared for a replacement. The interim tasks devolved upon the lieutenant governor, José Joaquín de Arrillaga, who served from the far-off point of Loreto in Baja California. On the actual scene, the senior command was again assumed by José Argüello.

At the time of the arrival of the *Sutil* and *Mexicana* in late September 1792, Roméu's widow was still present in California awaiting government transportation to remove her, her family, and her husband's adjutant, Pérez Hernández. The brief frontier assignment had not created in them any attachment for Monterey.

---

[12] Lasuén to Fr. Pablo de Mugártegui, San Carlos, April 10, 1792, in Kenneally, *Writings of Lasuén* 1 : 245–46.

Though California was a remote frontier province, and consequently it was difficult to recruit settlers to emigrate there from more-developed areas of New Spain, this isolation did not prevent meritorious candidates from seeking the vacant governorship. Shortly before the arrival of the *Sutil* and *Mexicana* the news of Roméu's death had brought forth the candidacy of at least four men, any one of whom might have merited such an appointment. They were Manuel de Echeagaray, Pedro Alberni, Francisco Antonio Mourelle, and Diego de Borica, all of whom petitioned or had petitions made on their behalf. "The Quest for the Governorship of Spanish California," [13] as Manuel Servin has appropriately called it, brings forth in its supporting documentation some information and insights on the area during the early 1790s.

Of the four candidates, all had persuasive facts buttressing their causes. Manuel de Echeagaray was commanding officer of the Presidio de Santa Cruz in Sonora. He was a veteran of the Apache campaigns on that frontier and had commanded an exploratory expedition seeking a practical trade route between the provinces of Sonora and New Mexico. His cause was espoused by his father, a resident of Mexico City.

Lieutenant Colonel Pedro Alberni was a member of the Catalonian Volunteers, a unit closely associated with the protection and advance of the northern frontier. At the time of Roméu's death, Alberni was stationed at Nootka as military commander of the army detachment there. In a letter of June 26, 1792, his cause was advanced by his wife, Juana Vélez y Carrera, then a resident in Guadalajara. Had all of Alberni's merits been known at the time, his candidacy would have had greater weight. Alberni had been recruited originally for the Portuguese campaigns, after which he was transferred to the New World, where he served successively in Sonora, Nayarit, and Nootka. While in the latter station he had made significant contributions, introducing European agriculture, strengthening relations with the local Indians, aiding visiting scientists, and constructing the buildings of the Spanish post

---

[13] Manuel P. Servin, "The Quest for the Governorship of Spanish California," in *California Historical Society Quarterly* 43, no. 1 (March 1964): 45–46.

there. At Nootka he was visited by and rendered considerable assistance to Malaspina in 1791 and to the *Sutil* and *Mexicana* in 1792 before their circumnavigation of Vancouver Island.

Much of that activity was contemporary with the interest of Alberni's wife in his advancement, but was not yet known to her. Though Alberni's quest was unsuccessful in 1792, his future service took him to California after the Spanish left Nootka. In California he was instrumental in founding the third and last Spanish civil settlement, the Villa de Branciforte, adjacent to Mission Santa Cruz. In 1800, upon the death of the governor, Alberni became senior military commander and therefore acting governor of California for a short time.[14]

The cause of the third candidate, Francisco Antonio Mourelle de la Rúa, was certainly much better represented because he was a special assistant to the viceroy in matters concerning Nootka, and because editing diaries of Pacific Coast exploration had made him more cognizant of California affairs. Of the four candidates, he knew the most about the area, both from firsthand contact and from his perusal of secondhand accounts. It is hard to assign a logical reason for his failure to be appointed. Based either on his merits, as reflected in a fulsome petition on July 30, 1792, or on his subsequent highly successful career, he was an attractive candidate. Possibly it was his non-naval-academy training. He had come up the hard way with seven years in the pilot corps before he bridged the chasm between that and a regular navy commission. This negative factor was largely nullified by his earlier induction as a military knight of the highly prestigious Order of Santiago. Another negative might have been a lack of confidence that Malaspina had in Mourelle. Originally Viceroy Revilla Gigedo had

[14] Donald C. Cutter, "Pedro de Alberni y los primeros experimentos de agricultura científica en la costa noroueste del Pacífico," *Revista de Historia Naval* 5 (1987), no. 18. A probable negative factor bearing on Alberni's candidacy for the governorship of California was his earlier poor relationship with the president of the Audiencia of Guadalajara. In defense of his troops, he was reportedly outspoken to the point of offensiveness. He was officially censured, and when he left for Nootka, he was under technical arrest. Furthermore, he departed without bidding an official farewell to his immediate superior.

planned to send the single vessel, the *Mexicana,* on the 1792 sortie to explore the inland passage.[15] Instead, as mentioned earlier, Malaspina had been insistent that Mourelle be replaced and that the *Sutil* and *Mexicana,* under Dionisio Alcalá Galiano and Cayetano Valdés, be sent to carry out the important last search for a Spanish Northwest Passage. Malaspina argued that, despite Mourelle's great sailing experience, his sufficiency of pilotage skills, "and his resolve and enthusiasm capable of the greatest things," the Gallego's ill health and his lack of mastery of sophisticated nautical instruments, and therefore his incapacity to take accurate latitudes and longitudes, worked together to make Mourelle's appointment less desirable.[16] Thus, Mourelle was not selected despite his advantageous position in the viceregal court near the source of decision making and his eighteen years of service in the Naval Department of San Blas including trips to the Philippines and China, as well as participation in several of the earliest Spanish voyages to the Pacific Northwest Coast.

Mourelle's interesting petition sheds light on not only the early phases of a noteworthy naval career but also contemporary California conditions. It reflects something that Mourelle was perhaps more aware of than anyone else—the lack of geographical knowledge of the province. Mourelle advanced his exploratory expertise as an asset, saying that with his appointment, "the exploration of those neighboring coasts and even of the distant ones (when Your Excellency should order that they be examined from land), the investigation of the inland territories, the location and true position of the large rivers that flow through them, and all the geographical descriptions which to this day we do not possess, could be accomplished without expense to the royal treasury in such a case."[17] He also referred to early proposals for economic development and the need for protection of Spanish interests in the fur

[15] Revilla Gigedo to Conde de Lerena, México, November 22, 1791, in Malaspina Correspondencia, 3, MS 280 in MN.

[16] Revilla Gigedo to Malaspina, México, November 22, 1791, in Malaspina Correspondencia, 3, MS 280 in MN.

[17] Servin, "Quest for the Governorship," p. 49.

trade, where operations were prejudiced by foreigners who inevitably would cause harm.

Mourelle's future and his greatest successes did not lie in the Pacific Ocean nor even in the Americas. He was soon back in Spain, where he participated gallantly in the defense of Algeciras and in combat against the British as well as the French. Promoted regularly, Mourelle reached the rank of *jefe de escuadra* (rear admiral) and in 1820 was given command of an abortive effort by Spain to recover its overseas possessions that had been in rebellion since 1810. His Gran Expedición de Ultramar never got underway. It was a last futile effort to try to stamp out the Greater American Revolution, with the target area the United Provinces of the Rio de la Plata.[18]

In retrospect, perhaps Mourelle's long service at sea and his lack of shore duty had made him more apt to be considered for preferment in naval assignments than in an essentially army-controlled military government post such as the governorship of California. His subsequent career and his final resting place in the Pantheon of Illustrious Mariners near Cádiz suggest that he might well have been a good choice for governor of California.[19]

The successful candidate in the pursuit of California's command was Lieutenant Colonel Diego de Borica y Retegui, another experienced officer. By the date of his petition he had over twenty-nine years of service divided between infantry and cavalry assignments. He was serving as adjutant inspector of the Interior Provinces of New Spain, a command that included all the northern provinces except California. Much of Borica's activity had been in Nueva Vizcaya with frequent duty in or visits to New Mexico. His combat experience against Apaches and Comanches, his reviews and inspections of presidios, his work with militia units, and his service in frontier defensive organization were all advanced as merit criteria. Most recently, just before his June 20, 1792, petition written

[18] Donald C. Cutter, "California, Training Ground for Spanish Naval Heroes," California Historical Society *Quarterly* 40, no. 2 (June 1961): 109–22.

[19] Mourelle died at Cádiz on May 24, 1820. Much material exists concerning his activities. Particularly interesting are Notas del Don Francisco Mourelle, MS 999 in MN.

from Chihuahua City, he had been commissioned to inform the viceroyalty of the state of the Interior Provinces:

> In '89, '90, '91, and part of the present year, he [Borica] was commissioned to visit the Tarahumaras, the Tepehuanes, the Spanish settlements, mining towns, haciendas, and ranchos of Nueva Vizcaya in order to apprehend all classes of offenders, and to introduce measures benefitting the Indians living in the pueblos. This he carried out, apprehending many criminals, pardoning those who voluntarily gave themselves up, and removing the extremely grave oppressions suffered by the Indians who numbered 33,500 individuals of every class who were living in seventy-five pueblos.[20]

Borica asserted that he had logged a travel record of 9,500 leagues, or about 25,000 miles, on horseback in campaigns and on official business trips. Borica had command experience in the field and a strong record of achievement. Since 1783 he, too, had been a Knight of the Order of Santiago. Based on the foregoing reasons, Borica became governor of California in 1794, the first of three consecutive Basque governors who led the province's development during the late Spanish period. Colonel Borica served as governor until his death six years later in 1800.

While awaiting the arrival of the soon-to-be-appointed replacement for Roméu, Lieutenant Governor Arrillaga delegated the command of local affairs to the most senior of the army officers present in Upper California, José Argüello, who was the local officer in command of Monterey Presidio both at the time of Malaspina's visit in September 1791 and at the time of the visit of Alcalá Galiano and Valdés in 1792. Argüello's efforts were appreciated by both groups of visitors, and he was appropriately commended, even to the point of being mentioned by name in the final report of the Malaspina expedition. That naval explorer's appreciation was also expressed in a letter that he wrote to the not-yet-arrived Governor Roméu, in which Malaspina said: "I cannot fail to make known to you . . . the effective help for which the expedition is endebted to the lieutenant of this [Monterey] company,

[20] Servin, "Quest for the Governorship," pp. 53–54.

Don Josef Arguellos [*sic*]. It has been as prompt and active as we could desire, and thus it obliges me to recommend said officer with the greatest efficacy." [21]

In the previously mentioned petition for the governorship, Naval Lieutenant Francisco Antonio Mourelle touched upon several interesting topics of contemporary and future importance for the young province. His suggestion of ridding the California coast of clandestine traders, who also engaged in poaching of what Spain considered, not illogically, to be its natural resources, is a very early recognition of what was to become a primary concern during the next quarter century. If prior to this there had been illegal trade contacts with the presidios and missions, nothing is known of them, this petition being the first substantiation. It is possible that Mourelle was giving the province elastic northern limits by extending California to include the maximum extent of Spanish naval explorations in the Pacific Northwest. If so, it would be easier to determine just who the interlopers were to whom he referred in his petition.

The coast provided two attractions for non-Spaniards: the fur business (consisting of the capture of, or trade for, valuable pelts) and the opening of general trade with the California settlements. By Spanish standards neither activity was legal, though Spain's pretensions to exclusive sovereignty in the Pacific were the subject of a serious challenge, with Spain in a deteriorating diplomatic position. The protracted Nootka Sound Controversy over the respective rights of Spain and Great Britain in the entire Pacific Ocean area, and more particularly on the Northwest Coast, found Spain for the first time strongly challenged. Before a final admission of diplomatic defeat, Spain was seeking the least humiliating solution. Without attempting to go into the merits of the dispute, it is enough to know that the regional solution involved implementation of a decision made thousands of miles from the point of friction. It was in defense of Spain's position that first Malaspina and subsequently the *Sutil*

[21] Malaspina to Roméu, Corvette Descubierta in the Bay of Monterey, September 24, 1791, in Apuntes, noticias y correspondencia pertenecientes a la espedición de Malaspina, MS 427 in MN.

and *Mexicana* were ordered to visit the northern latitudes. Otherwise Malaspina would have visited the Hawaiian Islands as he had originally intended to do, and the visit of the *Sutil* and *Mexicana* would never have been thought of. Not only was obscure Nootka Sound placed in the spotlight of international relations, but also Monterey, as a point of refreshment and recuperation, became a port of call for both Spanish and British vessels engaged in implementation of poorly understood instructions that suffered from the imprecision that distance often lends to such things.

Though Spain had never as yet been seriously interested in the fur trade and had no European tradition of such activity, California's lack of export items of small weight and great value resulted in unanticipated action. The geographical position of California and the resources of the coast could not be totally overlooked. Valuable sea otter abounded from Trinidad Head southward over the hundreds of miles of shoreline of both Upper and Lower California. Even if few of the local Indians had nautical skills, and even if they had no prior interest in fur gathering, these were attitudes that could be developed in time. The existence along the coast of countless abalone highly favored the trading aspect of the fur business because the shells had a primary place in the trade. They seem to have been one of the few trade items that held their value when brought to the Pacific Northwest Coast, another focal point of the fur trade. The beautiful, nacre-encrusted shells were available particularly in the vicinity of Monterey. Gathering them took minimal skill, and their weight and volume were small in comparison to their value. Spanish control of the source of these shells was an advantage easily appreciated. Not only did Spain envision using these shells in trade, it wanted to deny access to them to outsiders.

Because the fur trade was not necessarily a government activity, it was an economic area where the private sector of the colonial economy could become involved. Bureaucratic Spain, still much too top-heavy administratively despite recent reforms, spent considerable time pondering the fur business. Plans for a government-authorized monopoly of such economic activity generated plentiful documentation, much of which can be found today, particularly in the Archivo General de Indias.[22] The requested monopolies included exclusive control of fur collection along the Pacific Coast, transport of such furs to the great Oriental market aboard the Manila galleon sailing from Acapulco, acquisition of mercury from China as a return cargo to be sold in the silver-mining areas of Mexico, and a share in the California supply business that normally was channeled through the Nayarit coastal port of San Blas. A frequent favor seeker, Vicente Vasadre y Vega, had a half decade earlier been granted such a monopoly, but his efforts in implementing it never achieved enough success to permit him to continue as sole exploiter. Vasadre's plan, with modifications and with proposed leadership in other hands, was revived by José Pérez de Tagle, San Blas chef Nicolás Manzanelli, and Spanish naval officer Estevan José Martínez. Of all of these, only the first, Vasadre, ever actually shipped furs to the China market, and this was on three separate occasions.

In 1791, Malaspina showed his interest in the fur trade by collecting pertinent documents. The naval scientist recognized the infeasibility of such plans, but at the same time gathered documents illustrative of the proposed role of the California Franciscans and the Lower California Dominicans.[23] In 1790, Governor Fages had promulgated regulations that were of interest.[24] In 1791 the Vasadre contract was canceled, leading to a full-scale investigation the following year. Shortly thereafter the impetus for government involvement in the fur trade was lost. It would be hard to establish Malaspina's responsibility for termination of the monopoly, but he was certainly opposed to it, and he had the ear of the viceroy in Mexico City. At the time of the 1792 visit to Monterey there had been no further action on the matter.

The arrival of foreign traders and poachers, soon to become fully

[22] AGI *legajos* containing plans for fur-trade development include Audiencia de Guadalajara 493 and 494 and Audiencia de México 1523, 1548, and 1563.

[23] Extracto de lo que ha ocurrido en las negociaciones de pieles de nutria emprendidos desde el año 1784 in Reino de México, tomo 3, MS 335 in MN.

[24] Fages to José Francisco de Ortega, Monterey, September 13, 1790, and Fages's order of September 9, 1790, both in Malaspina Correspondencia, 2, MS 279 in MN.

evident, brought an end to all such Spanish fur-trade plans. What Mourelle had predicted in his petition for the governorship came to pass. For immediate returns, it became easier for locals to sell their furs to furtive ship captains at unfrequented bays along the coast than to go through legal channels fraught with fur-deteriorating delays and slow payoffs. The temptation, yielded to by persons of all categories, made government monopoly or private control of the fur trade an impossibility. Spain's position was even worse because the long California shoreline made it impossible to patrol against smugglers from abroad and their confederates within. The bottom line was that through lack of positive, aggressive action Spain did not profit appreciably from its geographical position. Foreign nations were soon dominant despite longer supply lines, less secure markets, and limited financial investment. Spain had failed to take advantage of its long-standing Pacific Ocean trade route, its physical presence on the coast, and its capacity to tap the China market at the port of Canton. Spain was no longer able to offer competition in a very competitive field.

Another contemporary subject introduced by Mourelle in his application for elevation to the provincial governorship in 1792 was the lack of satisfactory geographical knowledge not only of the coastal areas but also of the great valley known to lie east of the settled coastal fringe. In 1792 the streams feeding San Francisco Bay and its tributary bays to the northeast were largely unknown. Mourelle, a naval officer and an experienced pilot, indicated that if promoted to the regional command he would explore those bodies of water and ascertain the true nature and course of the Rio San Francisco (the Sacramento–San Joaquin river system). Such knowledge as existed was restricted to the early tentative efforts to reach the north shore of the bay at the time of its initial discovery. In 1776, Lieutenant Juan de Ayala had entered the bay with the *San Carlos,* and he and Lieutenant José Cañizares had explored and mapped the main bay areas, but its tributary rivers were still unknown. Early in his California career as a lieutenant, Pedro Fages had discovered the southern end of the San Joaquin Valley and had also visited the extreme western edge of the delta of the combined rivers. He was the first to recognize the great extent of the Central Valley's San Joaquin end.

There existed the as-yet-unquenched hope that the river system might be sufficiently extensive to lead a long way toward a desired goal—direct contact with the ancient province of New Mexico.[25] Contemporary with these early western approaches were the travels of the peripatetic Aragonese Franciscan Father Francisco Garcés, who had entered the southern end of the San Joaquin Valley and from there made his way to the western reaches of New Mexico. In turn, Garcés had stimulated the well-known expedition of Fathers Silvestre Vélez de Escalante and Francisco Domínguez. Trying to bridge the long, but as yet unknown, distance to California, the two priests left New Mexico and got only as far as central Utah. In collaboration with their mapmaker, Bernardo de Miera y Pacheco, and stimulated by misunderstood Indian informants, they created the mythical Rio Bonaventura. This "stream," which appeared on many maps, flowed from Utah to empty into San Francisco Bay and became a geographical legend of long duration.

Years had passed and the great valley had been left untouched. The knowledge of it that was conveyed to Malaspina in 1791 was certainly imperfect, for he based his native population estimates on the "positive surety that New California is populated regularly along the seashore only."[26] Obviously, he had been the victim of inadequate sources of information.

There had been total inaction concerning interior exploration, nor had there been any recent attempts to ascend the "Rio de San Francisco." Nor did Mourelle's petition awaken any interest. Another decade and a half would pass before any significant inland reconnaissance was carried out. Malaspina, Alcalá Galiano, and Valdés were not interested in California's hinterland, nor could they have logically been expected to initiate such activity. Save for the unfulfilled instruction to put in at San Francisco, the officers of the *Sutil* and *Mexicana* were largely unconcerned with the long-

[25] Donald C. Cutter, "Spanish Exploration of California's Central Valley," Ph.D. diss., University of California, Berkeley, 1950, pp. 3–28.

[26] Malaspina, Descripción de la California, MS 621 in MN.

standing geographical questions with regard to the hinterland. Cardero did copy a map of San Francisco Bay, originally done by San Blas pilot Juan de Pantoja, to which the artist added the touch of a chapel placed at the site of Mission San Francisco de Assisi. The Pantoja map, though it had considerable detail, did not add any information concerning the interior.

An obvious question concerns the impact that the visit of the *Sutil* and *Mexicana* had on California. There is almost no significant reference to either the 1792 visit or the earlier visit of Malaspina's group; the local archives are of little help concerning the visit or the visitors. This can be explained because there was no reason why local authorities, for example, Father Lasuén and senior military commander Argüello, would feel obliged to report about the explorer-scientists and their visit. The exploratory groups were logically the reporters while the local residents were occasional subjects of such investigations. The Spanish crown had sent top-level investigators, who, with considerable local assistance, had made such inquiries as were called for by their instructions. Other scientific visitors to California on somewhat similar missions, such as Jean François Galaup de La Pérouse, Nicolai Rezanof, and George Vancouver, generated greater quantities of local documentation not because they were more important but because the Spanish monarch was not going to receive any reports from such foreign visitors and it was of interest to know what such sojourners were doing.

Malaspina in 1791 and the *Sutil* and *Mexicana* mariners of 1792 did not report as extensively on Upper California as they did on most other areas that they visited. Doubtless, they realized that such information was routinely reported through normal channels. They also knew that local events, almost as they happened, were being reported beyond their capacity to illumine such occurrences. Selectivity rather than comprehensiveness was the result, whether purposely or accidentally. Rest and recuperation were important considerations in both 1791 and 1792 in the brief California stops, though even "recreation" served useful ends such as fishing, botanizing, observing, and doing other fieldwork to advance the expedition agenda.

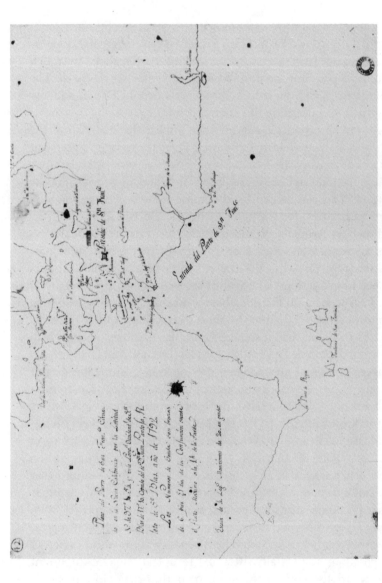

José Cardero's copy of Juan de Pantoja's map of the port of San Francisco (*Plano del Puerto de San Fran[co] cituado en la Nueva California . . . , 1792*). Museo Naval.

3. Dramatis Personae

Commanding Officers

Neither of the young commanding officers of the two small schooners that put into Monterey in September 1792 probably felt strongly that the stop there was of any significance either historically or in their career objectives. Both were young, vigorous, and talented mariners with important careers ahead of them. One died a young hero and the other lived to a venerable, highly honored old age. That originally they had been selected to accompany Malaspina is evidence of their standing among contemporary junior naval officers. It was evidence of their potential future status that Malaspina had selected them to carry out the last search for the Strait of Anian.

The national publicity surrounding the larger voyage, with frequent official correspondence at the highest levels of naval, viceregal, and ministerial administration, made the two officers' names known at an age when most young officials were not yet recognized. Also, it could only have enhanced the chances of success for Cayetano Valdés and his close associates that Valdés's uncle, Antonio Valdés y Bazán, was minister of marine, the administrative head of the Spanish Navy. Nepotism has frequently given a considerable boost to the careers of both the deserving and the undeserving.

Cayetano Valdés y de Flores was born on September 28, 1767,

in Sevilla on a street that was later renamed Calle Almirante Valdés.[1] His family was from Asturias (specifically, from San Román de Candamo) and was quite prominent in governmental affairs. At age fourteen Cayetano obtained appointment as a midshipman at the naval school at Cádiz. A year later he saw his first of many military actions, on this occasion under Admiral Luis de Córdoba against the British under Admiral Richard Howe off the Strait of Gibraltar. Subsequently, under Admiral Antonio Barceló, Valdés took part in nine naval engagements in the struggle for Argel on the North African coast. To this was added two visits to Constantinople and service under Admiral Vicente Tofiño in the great mapping project of Spain. By 1789, when he was chosen to accompany Malaspina's naval scientific exploring expedition, he was already a senior-grade lieutenant.

For two years Valdés served with distinction under the command of Alejandro Malaspina during the first half of the famous voyage, earning promotion to commander. During his first visit to California with Malaspina in 1791, Valdés was given charge of a salvage detail attempting to recover three anchors which had been lost during a difficult entry into the harbor of Monterey. In that effort he commanded two launches and a small schooner, the *Santa Saturnina* (34-¾ tons), which had been commandeered for the purpose. The attempt met with failure owing to bad weather, poor visibility, and limited available time.[2]

After the 1792 visit that is the subject of this study, Valdés disembarked in San Blas and made his way back to Spain via Mexico City and Veracruz, arriving finally in Cádiz on June 11,

---

[1] Except as otherwise noted, the following sketch of Cayetano Valdés's life is an abbreviated summary of several available biographical sources. These include Francisco de Paula Pavia, *Galería biográfica de los generales de marina,* vol. 3 (Madrid, 1873, pp. 697–712; Historial de los servicios de los Capitanes generales que tubo la Armada, MS 1193 in MN; Expediente personal of Cayetano Valdés y Florez in Archivo-Museo Alvaro de Bazán (AMAB), El Viso del Marqués; and Cutter, "California, Training Grounds for Spanish Naval Heroes," p. 119.

[2] Cutter, *Malaspina in California,* pp. 34–35; Viage en Limpio de las Corbetas Descubierta y Atrevida, MS 181 in MN.

1793, aboard the naval vessel *Cazador*.[3] The following year Valdés was promoted to captain, achieving that advanced rank while only twenty-seven years old. In Spain, Valdés was assigned to Cartagena Naval Department and given command of the naval vessel *San Fulgencio,* in which he went to Italy. Later, from 1796 to 1801, he was in command of the warship *Pelayo* in Admiral José de Córdoba's fleet, and was commended for saving the flagship *Trinidad* from falling into the hands of the British. In 1799, still on the *Pelayo,* Valdés was promoted to command of the first division of the first squadron of the Spanish fleet. Shortly thereafter he served as major general of the Spanish squadron for the international force mobilized at Brest in France, an abortive cooperative operation that had the invasion of England as its goal. From Brest, Valdés went to Havana and then to Cádiz.

Both Valdés and Alcalá Galiano took part in one of history's great naval battles off Cape Trafalgar in October 1805. In a losing cause, Valdés fought gallantly from the decks of the warship *Neptuno* (80 guns, 800 crew), which was demasted, captured, recovered, and finally brought into Cádiz Bay, where, to prevent capture by the enemy, it was sunk on the coast at Puerto Santa María, opposite Cádiz. In that famous battle Valdés was seriously wounded, and he was later promoted to *jefe de escuadra* as a reward for his bravery. The promotion also gained him command of the Mediterranean Squadron with headquarters at Cartagena.

During the uneasy days of the Napoleonic invasion of Spain, with the establishment of the regency at Cádiz, Valdés played an increasingly political role as a liberal. As lieutenant general he was governor, captain general, and political chief of Cádiz. Because he was a man of liberal political ideas, when absolute government was reestablished in 1814, Valdés suffered. He was sent for confinement in the Castillo de Santa Bárbara, the ancient fortification atop Monte Benacantil which still dominates the Alicante sector of the western Mediterranean. During the six years of an original eight-

---

[3] Lista de oficiales agregados a la compañia de Guardias Marinas: Año de 1792, MS 1099 in MN.

year sentence that he spent there, he had many opportunities to gaze out to sea and once in a while to think of a happier day when as a youthful commander he had carried the colors of Spain into uncharted waters along the Pacific Northwest Coast. During his incarceration Valdés was informed that he would be restored to full royal favor by King Fernando VII if he would beg for a royal pardon, which he emphatically refused to do, feeling that such an action on his part would be an admission of guilt.

Valdés's imprisonment was not totally unpleasant. He received full pay, could go to the nearby bathing beaches, ride horseback, and even have a room in town. While a prisoner, he was ordered to detached duty to make an official inspection of naval affairs at Cartagena, and having done so, he returned to his incarceration. Shortly thereafter, he requested and received royal permission to marry, which implies that he had sufficient liberty to carry out a successful courtship. According to the records of Santa María Church in Alicante, his bride was Isabel Roca de Togores, widow of a defunct naval officer, Francisco Valcarcel y Pio de Saboya.

In a kaleidoscopic turn of events, Valdés was restored to his previous position in Cádiz. When the French Count of Angoulême invaded Spain from the north, Valdés formed part of the regency named to transport Fernando VII from Sevilla to Cádiz. He was also one of the petitioners to the Cortes asking that the king be deposed and thus stripped of his political powers. For a brief period of three days, Valdés was part of a regency governing Spain, one that renounced its powers once Fernando was installed in Cádiz, where he planned to rule as a constitutional monarch. In the defense of Cádiz against the French, Valdés was in command of both the land and sea forces.

In the rapidly shifting course of events, the royal family was transported across the bay to the enemy general headquarters at Puerto de Santa María, and Valdés commanded the boat on that assignment. En route the king forgave him their differences, but later that same night the sovereign signed a decree ordering the apprehension and execution of Valdés among others who had taken part in the Junta of Cádiz. With his life in danger, and despite being a deputy to the Cortes and president of the Deputación Permanente, Valdés was not seen again in Spain for many years after the fateful launch trip across Cádiz Bay. He had received an offer from the French commander that effectively banished him. As a result, Valdés took refuge in British Gibraltar and from there went to England. He was reportedly very well treated. He might well have reflected back to three decades earlier when he and English mariners were cooperating as friendly rivals in an exploratory search for the Northwest Passage.

Fernando VII finally died, and an amnesty decree was promulgated in Spain. Consequently, Don Cayetano returned home and was immediately made captain general of the navy and head of the Naval Department of Cádiz. He was also named a grandee of the kingdom, and he retained all of these honors until his death. In addition to those appointments, he had received several important decorations during his earlier career.

Valdés's death, of natural causes, occurred in Cádiz on February 6, 1835, with subsequent burial in the nearby Catholic cemetery of San Fernando. Years later a royal decree of June 11, 1851, ordered his reburial in the not-yet-completed Pantheon of Illustrious Mariners. Because of the unfinished status of the pantheon, Valdés's remains were not moved until October 2, 1858, and were deposited "in a wooden box in an unkept chapel" under the command of the captain general of Cádiz. At some unspecified date after 1860, the final transfer of Valdés's remains was effected, and in one of the simplest of the graves in that naval shrine his final resting place was established beneath a stone that reads:

Here lies the Most Excellent Lord
Don Cayetano Valdés y Flores
former Captain General of the National Navy
Knight of the Great Cross of the Military Orders
of San Fernando, San Hermenegildo, and that of
San Juan de Jerusalem [4]

[4] Another source, Fallecidos 1809–1824, MS 1256 in MN, gives the place of Valdés's death as Madrid. Concerning his final burial see José A. Berrocal Garrido, *El Panteón de Ilustres Marinos* (Cádiz, 1890), pp. 62, 109, 120–21.

Cayetano Valdés, commanding officer of the *Mexicana*. Museo Naval, Madrid.

The life of Dionisio Alcalá Galiano is also of interest. He is still known as a hero and martyr.[5] In the original operation plan of the Malaspina expedition, Don Dionisio's name was not included, but shortly thereafter he became a substitute for the unavailable Ventura Barcaiztegui. He lived up to the great expectations of his commander, who even before their initial departure rated Alcalá Galiano as irreplaceable.[6] For the remainder of his life "the talent and hard-working character of Alcalá Galiano" stood out as early predicted.[7]

Born in Cabra in Andalusia on October 8, 1760, Dionisio de Alcalá-Galiano y de Alcalá-Galiano was the son of a regimental colonel based in Ecija.[8] The son, Dionisio, became a midshipman at Cádiz, probably in July 1775. At an early age, as a junior officer, he was associated with notable naval figures. He first embarked on the frigate *Jupiter* in 1776. When General Pedro de Ceballos left Spain to become viceroy in Buenos Aires on November 13, 1777, Alcalá Galiano was a junior officer in the 116-vessel convoy entrusted to the Marqués de Casa Tilly. While in South America, Alcalá Galiano participated in the Spanish capture of Colonia de Sacramento (now in Uruguay), which was taken in war from the Portuguese and was kept under the terms of the Treaty of San Ildefonso of February 1778. Also on this tour of overseas duty, Alcalá Galiano spent about two years in the Malvinas (Falkland) Islands, an area that he later visited as a member of the Malaspina

[5] Except as otherwise noted, the following sketch of Dionisio Alcalá's life is a brief summary of available biographical sources. These include Pavia, *Galería Biográfica de los Generales de Marina* 1:47–57; Jaime Salvá, *Alcalá Galiano* (Cartagena, n.d.); Expediente personal of Dionisio Alcalá Galiano y Alcalá Galiano in AMAB; and Cutter, "California, Training Ground for Spanish Naval Heroes," pp. 118–19.

[6] A. Valdés to Malaspina, Madrid, February 3, 1789, in Malaspina Correspondencia, I, MS 278 in MN.

[7] Malaspina to A. Valdés, Montevideo, October 30, 1789, in Correspondencia relativa al viage de Malaspina . . . , MS 583 in MN.

[8] At baptism he was named Dionisio Francisco de Paula Benito de Santa Brigada de Jesús María y Josef Alcalá Galiano Alcalá Galiano Pareja Pinedo. It was noted that his parents were related in the fourth degree of consanguinity but had ecclesiastical permission for marriage. Ordenes Militares—Alcántara—Pruebas de Caballeros 42 in AHN.

expedition in 1789. Among other activities, Don Dionisio operated as a corsair and captured an English merchant frigate. Subsequently, he returned to Cádiz, where he undertook special studies in astronomy.

The year 1784 was spent by Alcalá Galiano working under the command of Admiral Tofiño in the great hydrographic study of the coasts of Spain, but in the following year Alcalá Galiano was again in South America as one of the officers engaged with Antonio de Córdoba in mapping the Straits of Magellan, another area that he revisited while with Malaspina. Either just before or just after this duty assignment, he married María de la Consolación Villavicencio, a relative from Medina Sidonia. By this marriage he had four children, three of whom were boys. One son, Antonio, who later became an important political figure, left behind some printed memoirs that shed light on his father's career and personality.[9] Early in his career Alcalá Galiano was characterized as "married, poor, and honorable, a man who would someday give his nation glory by his activities."[10] Unlike Valdés, Alcalá Galiano spent his entire career in naval assignments and was never involved in politics.

Before joining Malaspina, Dionisio had a season of mapping, again with Tofiño, on the coasts of Asturias and Vizcaya in northern Spain, serving aboard the *Loreto*. With Malaspina's round-the-world exploring expedition, Alcalá Galiano served with distinction and was promoted to commander in 1791, but he was not present when the corvettes visited California. While the corvettes were engaged in their cruise to Alaska, British Columbia, and California, Alcalá Galiano was sent from Acapulco to Mexico City to gather archival information and other documents useful for current and future expedition needs. In Mexico he also engaged in one of his specialties, astronomical observation, as well as working on geographical studies of Mexico and Central America.

[9] Antonio Alcalá Galiano was a politician, diplomat, and at one time minister of the Spanish Navy.

[10] Malaspina to A. Valdés, Montevideo, October 30, 1789, in Correspondencia relativa al viage de Malaspina . . . , MS 583 in MN.

Alcalá Galiano had ultimate responsibility as senior commander of the two-vessel task group made up of the *Sutil* and *Mexicana*, but from the extant documentation the impression is clear that both he and Valdés acted as equals. The two carried out an almost superhuman feat in coaxing the undersized, undermanned, and painfully slow schooners to sail some eight thousand miles in a single short season, a feat made even more remarkable because the sailing speed of the two tiny vessels was about seven knots.

Upon his return from the 1792 reconnaissance, Alcalá Galiano spent some time in Mexico City, where he presented his reports and maps to the viceroy and made certain required changes. After a short tour of duty in the Caribbean, he returned to Spain on September 5, 1794, on the naval vessel *San Isidro*, disembarking at Cádiz.[11] By October he was in Madrid, along with Juan Vernacci, to present the papers resulting from the commission to the Strait of Juan de Fuca. As a reward for his services, Alcalá Galiano was promoted to captain in the Spanish Navy. Another reward was granted on December 5, 1795, that of entry into the knighthood order of Alcántara.

Alcalá Galiano soon was scheduled to carry out a cherished plan for construction of a topographic map of the Iberian Peninsula, a project that failed to materialize. Meanwhile, he was busy with plans for publication of the account of the voyage of the schooners *Sutil* and *Mexicana*. However, instead of the rapid progress leading to publication that he anticipated, he was soon sent back to Cádiz. The cause was perhaps linked to his nearness to the now out-of-favor Malaspina. Dionisio was considered, not incorrectly, as a part of that officer's inner circle of men. Extant documentation indicates that Alcalá Galiano was doing his best to downplay any connection between the schooners and Malaspina's grand enterprise by claiming that his two-schooner command of 1792 was totally independent and that from the very beginning he had acted under the direct orders of Viceroy Revilla Gigedo, something that clearly was

[11] Lista de oficiales agregados a la compañia de Guardias Marinas: Año de 1794, MS 1100 in MN.

not the case but rather a subterfuge that led to the eventual publication of the account.[12]

In the war with England, Alcalá Galiano commanded the warship *Vencedor* and subsequently took command of the *San Fulgencio* on a trip to Cartagena in South America. He next visited Veracruz, from which he returned to Europe via Cuba, bringing with him much-needed silver bullion from the New World, funds badly needed to support the war effort. Using a little frequented sailing route, Alcalá Galiano arrived with his precious cargo at the infrequently used harbor of Santoña in Santander province.[13] His mission complete, he went to El Ferrol and from there returned to America, this time commanding the *San Pedro de Alcántara*. A second time, he loaded silver at Veracruz, went from there to Havana, but failing to find favorable winds for crossing the Atlantic, was forced to return to Havana. He was at that Cuban port when the Peace of Amiens was signed, temporarily concluding hostilities and permitting unimpeded transport of his precious cargo.

By 1802, Alcalá Galiano had returned to Cádiz, where he took command of the warship *Bahama*. He was first ordered to Naples as part of an important convoy dispatched to pick up a local princess, María Antonia Borbon Sicilia, daughter of Fernando IV, king of Naples. She was to be brought to Spain to marry the eighteen-year-old crown prince later to be Fernando VII. A delay in plans developed so that Alcalá Galiano's ship was diverted to Tunis to settle an international problem, a result of which was his manuscript report "Results of the Campaign to Tunis of the Warship *Bahama* in 1802."

Don Dionisio rejoined the nuptual fleet headed for Naples. From that port the *Bahama* sailed to Barcelona with part of the royal entourage aboard. Alcalá Galiano was in his glory, being a man described as very given to ostentation and liberality, so much so that at the time of his death he left behind almost no estate and considerable debt.

---

[12] Alcalá Galiano to Pedro de Varela, Madrid, November 27, 1795, in Malaspina, 1788–1814, MS 2296 in MN.

[13] Alcalá Galiano is reported to have brought bullion in the amount of $7 million.

As a result of much royal generosity of the moment, Don Dionisio was promoted to brigadier (commodore), though he was not pleased with advancements made virtually across the board rather than on the basis of individual merit. Given command of the warship *Soledad,* he was sent to Greece and Constantinople on a project to map the eastern Mediterranean. There he spent about a year, after which he went to Madrid to publish his maps, and to Cádiz to write up the report of his voyage to the Levant.

Don Dionisio's last command was reassignment to the *Bahama.* In the famous Battle of Trafalgar pitting the British fleet of Lord Horatio Nelson against the combined Spanish and French fleets off the southwest coast of Spain, Alcalá Galiano's *Bahama* was overpowered by first two and then three British warships. In the exchange of naval gunfire Brigadier Alcalá Galiano was shot through the head by cannon fire, after which he was quickly buried at sea. Many others died in the same engagement on October 21, 1805, including the victor, British Admiral Nelson.

Of the 1792 visitors to California, Alcalá Galiano is the only one concerning whom we have a contemporary description and character assessment. He was described as studious and hardworking. He was short of stature with a rough and robust constitution; light in complexion, with blue eyes. He had a disagreeable look, like a disattentive person. He was of irascible temperament, rigid in the observance of discipline, exceedingly active, excessively generous, easily offended even over little things, and somewhat vain concerning his talents. His education was no greater than average. Even in the sciences, he knew perfectly well whatever he knew but his general knowledge was limited. He understood Latin moderately well; he translated and spoke French well; and he knew a little English. Of that little bit he bragged a great deal and was very proud because in his time the English language was very little known in Spain. He was also very loved by his subordinates.[14]

Alcalá Galiano's death at age forty-five with the rank of com-

---

[14] Dionisio Alcalá Galiano's son, Antonio, source of the character assessment paraphrased above, at no time made any claim for his father having been the author of the "Relación" of 1792, nor did he credit any other person with its composition.

Dionisio Alcalá Galiano, commanding officer of the *Sutil*. Museo Naval.

modore suggests that, had he lived and escaped the pitfalls of governmental change and the irrational dictates of an insecure monarch, he might well have equaled or surpassed the career of Cayetano Valdés, who outlived him by thirty years. His principal fame rests on the merit of martyrdom because he gave his life for his country in an historic battle. For this he has been commemorated in poetry, in naval history, and in patriotic Spanish writings. He was also the only participant aboard the *Sutil* or *Mexicana* to have any of his written work published. This publication was in the form of technical treatises on astronomy and navigation. It is also possible that he was the principal author of the account of the 1792 reconnaissance.

Seconds in Command

Not only were the senior visitors, Alcalá Galiano and Valdés, apt candidates for future advancement, but also the seconds in command, the only two other commissioned officers aboard the schooners, earned later advancement. The two were Juan Vernacci Retamal of Cádiz and Secundino Salamanca y Humara, born in Burgos. Both officers were reported to have served well on the expedition of 1792, a fact of particularly great importance because of the limited crew. As regards the range of service, Salamanca later wrote that "the four officers were required to carry out the functions of pilots, naturalists, artists, accountants, storekeepers, and others from the most sublime to the most routine." [15]

Juan Vernacci, as he spelled his Italian surname, though others rendered it in a variety of ways, was born in 1763. His father had also been born in the "white city" of Cádiz. His paternal grandfather, Raniero Vernacci, linked the family to Pisa, which was a possible reason for Malaspina's choice of Juan Vernacci as a "fellow Italian." The other side of Vernacci's family were Andalusians from San Lucar de Barrameda at the mouth of the Guadalquivir River.

Vernacci enlisted as a midshipman on September 13, 1780, and two years later received his initial commission as *alférez de fragata,* or ensign. A year later he was sublieutenant of the ninth brigade of midshipmen at the Cádiz naval training school. As was the case with many of the group later selected by Malaspina for his long cruise, Vernacci worked with Admiral Tofiño's great mapping project on the coasts of Spain. At twenty-nine he was chosen to join

[15] Petition of Vernacci and Salamanca, Madrid, November 5, 1794, in AMAB, Asuntos Personales, Juan Vernacci Retamal Villarelo.

Malaspina's naval scientific exploring expedition. During the two years that he served with the main group, he was particularly involved with astronomy, with checking the operation of the delicate, state-of-the-art, marine chronometers, and with cataloging the stars. Among the projects was that carried out with Lieutenant Juan Gutiérrez de la Concha of making a general map of the Argentine coasts.

While in California in 1792, Vernacci took a series of solar altitudes from the naval-supply storehouse on the beach at Monterey. Subsequently, he moved his astronomical headquarters to the presidio. Lacking further information, we can assume that, like the others, he dedicated himself to perfecting the rough notes, observations, and maps of the previous months of activity.

On the basis of Vernacci's participation aboard the *Mexicana,* and with the strong recommendation of his superiors, he was promoted simultaneously with Secundino Salamanca to lieutenant commander on March 24, 1795.[16] His later career also was involved with Alcalá Galiano, after the presentation and preparation for publication of the materials emanating from the voyage of the schooners. In 1796 both Juan and his brother, Joseph Vernacci, were placed under the command of Don Dionisio, but Juan first went to England to obtain navigational instruments.[17]

Later Vernacci was involved in combat duty, carried out mapping in Spain, and spent a year making astronomical studies at the naval observatory at Cádiz. A note indicates that in 1800 he participated in a campaign at Brest in France. A year later he commanded the nao *Magallanes* on a galleon run from Manila to Acapulco. From that time until the end of his life, Vernacci was associated with the Philippine Islands and, from time to time, with the interests of the Philippines Company, a semiofficial entity. In 1803 he was named to go via Coromandel and Bengal to

[16] A. Valdés to Antonio Ulloa, Aranjuez, March 24, 1795, in AMAB, Asuntos Personales, Vernacci.

[17] Notes of August 2 and 3, 1796, assigning the Vernacci brothers, Juan and Josef, to the command of Alcalá Galiano in AMAB, Asuntos Personales, Vernacci.

Manila to assume command of the "Acapulco vessel" in relief of its captain. In 1804, Vernacci participated in a hydrographic expedition during which he drew a map of the Philippine Islands Strait of San Bernardino.[18] Whether he returned at times from the Philippines or not is uncertain, but there is record of his death at Manila on January 4, 1810, at age forty-six while still holding the rank of *capitán de fragata,* or lieutenant commander.[19]

Secundino Salamanca, the *Sutil* subordinate commander, led a complicated life. Whereas Vernacci was involved almost exclusively in maritime pursuits, Salamanca's life was made complex by politics and by European power struggles.[20]

Salamanca was appointed midshipman at about age eighteen, probably based on his father's status, for José de Salamanca was a Knight of the Order of Santiago and governor of Villanueva de la Serena in Extremadura. Secundino was commissioned as *alférez de fragata* in 1784, but with the requirement that he pursue certain studies at midshipmen's school.[21] He saw service both with Admiral Juan de Lángara and with Admiral Tofiño in the Islas Terceras of the Azores. Salamanca received regular promotions, one just before his enlistment with Malaspina in 1789, when he was made *teniente de fragata.* In 1793 he was advanced to *teniente de navío* (lieutenant, senior grade), and later on the strength of a joint petition by Cayetano Valdés and Dionisio Alcalá Galiano on behalf of him and Vernacci, both men were made lieutenant commanders.[22]

When he returned to Spain after his association with the Malaspina command and his service aboard the *Sutil,* Salamanca was in

[18] José Vásquez Figueroa to Félix de Texada, Cádiz, January 30, 1812, in AMAB, Asuntos Personales, Vernacci.

[19] The death of Vernacci in Manila is noted in Oficiales 1821–1836, MS 1251 in MN.

[20] A fragmentary service record of Salamanca is in AMAB, Asuntos Personales, Secundino Salamanca.

[21] Salamanca's provisional appointment is indicated in Libro de Oficiales agregados . . . para estudios mayores, 1783, MS 1146 in MN.

[22] Petition in AMAB, Asuntos Personales, Vernacci, and seconded by Alcalá Galiano to A. Valdés, Madrid, December 13, 1794.

Cádiz. On June 13, 1793, he was sent to Madrid, where he served as a supernumerary officer attached to the Secretariat of the Navy.[23] The record shows Salamanca as discharged from the navy on November 13, 1803, but that must have been a temporary separation, because in 1805 he was promoted to full captain. In the interim he possibly served briefly in "the Americas," since his service record shows four years, five months, and six days of duty there, a length of time not consistent with his service there between 1789 and 1793.

In the year of his promotion to captain, 1805, Salamanca was sent to Admiral Federico Gravina's squadron as second-in-command of the warship *Rayo*. He, as well as Valdés and Alcalá Galiano, participated in the Battle of Trafalgar on October 21 of that year.

Salamanca was without assignment between 1806 and 1809, though in 1808 he was the subject of a complaint stemming from "evidence of his hatred of France." He had to go from Cádiz to Sevilla to defend himself, which he did satisfactorily before the captain general. He was nevertheless ordered to remain in Sevilla until further notice. His subsequent service record is even more jumbled, but includes a period as interim political and military governor of San Lucar de Barrameda. From 1811 until 1826, Secundino's name was no longer on the list of naval officers, and there was a note of his having taken refuge in France in 1813. It is also recorded that he made a trip to Philadelphia in 1816, becoming the only Malaspina veteran ever to visit the existing United States.

In 1826, Salamanca's name surfaces again when action was taken on his retirement without salary as a commodore. In the next year he was given half the salary of a commodore in lieu of a pension. Somewhere, according to his calculations, he had served in the Ministry of the Navy for fifteen years (possibly he counted much of the period from 1811 to 1826 to reach that figure). His death of natural causes is reported to have occurred in 1839 at age seventy-five.

[23] Salamanca's service record and occasional fugitive references have been utilized to summarize his career.

The Artist

José Cardero, artist and penman of the most extended version of the 1792 voyage of the schooners *Sutil* and *Mexicana,* is the participant who gained most from his association with that reconnaissance. Even before departure for the Northwest Coast he had improved his employment status and his pay considerably beyond that of his two years' service aboard the corvettes before his detachment to serve on the *Mexicana* during the summer of 1792. Of the five well-known members of the visiting team, Cardero's life story is the least accessible and cannot yet be fully told, though more details are now available than before. Compared to the sources for the biographical sketches of his commissioned companions, data concerning Cardero is much more scattered, never having been brought together previously.

Though the young Andalusian artist never used anything other than his first baptismal name, José (occasionally rendered Josef and Joseph) and his paternal surname of Cardero, his full name was José Antonio Feliciano Cardero Meléndez. In the archive of the parish church of Santa María and Santa Bárbara in Ecija his birth is recorded as follows:

> In the city of Ecija on Saturday, November 1, 1766, I, Andrés García, priest and curate of this parish church of Nuestra Señora Santa María, solemnly baptized José Antonio Feliciano, whom they said had been born on the past October 20, the son of Francisco Cardero and of María Meléndez, his legal wife. Alonso Pérez, a resident of this place, was godfather. I informed him of his spiritual relationship and obligation of teaching him the Christian faith, and I sign it
>
> Andrés García[24]

Cardero's name has been frequently miswritten Cordero, a much more common Spanish surname. This misspelling occurred often during his lifetime and has been perpetuated by modern and not-so-modern authors as a result of inattention and of repetition of

---

[24]Libro de Bautismos 26, f. 193v, MS.

equally careless secondary sources. It was also written as Caldero on at least two occasions by the equally careless chaplain of the *Descubierta,* Father José María de Mesa.

The Cardero family may have left Ecija, known as "the frying pan of Andalusia," as a result of its extreme summer temperatures, and moved to Cádiz on the more-benign Atlantic coast at some time before 1789. But of José's youth, his schooling, and his artistic training, if any, we have no record. An easy assumption is that he had formal education, because of his stylized and nearly flawless penmanship and his frequent role as amanuensis. His complete literacy places him well above the average educational development in his period. However, it did not result in a good initial appointment. To the contrary, at age twenty-three Cardero joined the Malaspina expedition in the lowly capacity of *criado,* the precise definition of which is difficult. Cabin boy, mess boy, page, orderly, and servant all come to mind. A long-standing association with Cayetano Valdés suggests that the young naval officer was a patron of Cardero, possibly having arranged his initial enlistment. It has been suggested that little "Pepe" Cardero was Valdés's personal servant, though this is not easily proved. Cardero did serve much of his seagoing career on the same vessel as Valdés, beginning on the *Descubierta* in 1789, then on the *Atrevida* in 1791, the *Mexicana* in 1792, and after their return to Spain, for a short time at Cartagena assigned to Valdés's vessel, the *San Fulgencio.* Though there is little doubt about a close bond, the nature of that relationship is unclear. Both were of similar ages, Valdés being two years senior. Both were Andalusians—Cardero from Ecija-Cádiz and Valdés from Sevilla-Cádiz. Furthermore, Cardero named his first son Cayetano, an uncommon Christian name and certainly no coincidence.[25]

Regardless of the circumstances of his enlistment, Cardero's name appears in the expedition documentation as "a servant of the officers," in a letter written from Guayaquil, Ecuador. At that point, when the corvettes had been fourteen months out of their

[25] Cardero to Principé de la Paz, La Carraca, November 4, 1806, Cuerpo de Ministerio, Asuntos Personales, José Cardero, in AMAB.

home port of Cádiz, Cardero first played a role worthy of a favorable note in the expedition record: "In the following days great progress was made with our natural history collection. They tried to make drawings of all the lesser-known species, toward which end José Cardero, servant of the officers, was very useful to us in everything that didn't directly concern botany." [26]

As Cardero continued in the role of de facto artist, his job description improved. While the expedition was at Panama, he was referred to as a "painter" in reference to his general views and his depiction of "interesting objects of natural history." [27] At the next stop, the shipbuilding port of Realejo, Nicaragua, Cardero was called a "dibuxante," a person who draws, if not yet an artist. [28] And since the *Atrevida* was on a parallel assignment elsewhere, the pictorial record from Realejo is completely the product of Cardero's efforts aboard the *Descubierta*.

At Acapulco on the southwestern coast of Mexico, Malaspina's expedition was strengthened by the addition of a Mexico City–based artist-engraver, Tomás de Suría, who started to work on expedition projects immediately. [29] Suría was officially an expedition artist on loan from the Mexican Mint through the good offices of Viceroy Revilla Gigedo. Even with Suría present, Cardero continued in his unofficial capacity as artist. While the expedition was still at Acapulco, staging for its Pacific Northwest Coast phase, a substantial shipment of boxes of specimens, maps, and drawings was sent to the Ministry of the Navy in Spain. Included were fifty-eight zoological drawings, of which Cardero had been responsible for forty-six. In addition, he was the artist of sixteen general views or perspectives emanating from already-completed visits to coastal ports. [30]

[26] Diarios 6, f. 100, in MS 276 in MN.
[27] Diarios 6, f. 129, in MS 276 in MN.
[28] Diarios 6, f. 155, in MS 276 in MN.
[29] Concerning Suría's participation see Donald C. Cutter, ed. and trans., *Journal of Tomás de Suría of His Voyage with Malaspina to the Northwest Coast of America in 1791* (Fairfield, Wash., 1980).
[30] Viaje alrededor del mundo, 1789–1796, MS 749 in MN, and Correspondencia relativa al viage de Malaspina, MS 583 in MN.

Cardero's association with Suría at Acapulco and during the Northwest Coast campaign is said by art historians to have influenced Cardero's techniques, thereby improving on his natural talent.[31] If so, this instruction was largely while they were yet at Acapulco, for once embarked, each on a different ship, the two men had only limited contact—ten days at Port Mulgrave at Yakutat Bay, Alaska, and two weeks each at Nootka Sound off Vancouver Island and at the California capital of Monterey. It was on the last stay that Cardero produced most of the drawings reproduced in this study, though it is vaguely possible that a few may have been done the second time that Cardero was in California, that is, while he was with the schooners *Sutil* and *Mexicana*.

In 1791, once Malaspina's vessels returned to Acapulco, both Suría and Cardero were surplus beyond the mission's requirements. Two highly recommended Italian artists, who had been contracted in Europe, had arrived in Mexico, where they were to intercept the exploratory party. They were Juan Ravenet and Fernando Brambila, who came as replacements for the deposed original artists, José del Pozo and José Guio.[32] Both of the Italians stayed with the expedition until its conclusion. Their arrival made it possible to send Suría back to the mint, from which he had been granted an open-ended leave of absence subject to right of reemployment.

Suría and Cardero's drawings "of the most important objects of the latest campaign" were sent to Spain. It was indicated on the shipping list that those done in pencil had been covered with glass so that they would not smear during shipment, though there seems to have been only one California item in pencil, with the title *Modo de Pelear de los Indios de California,* probably done by Cardero.[33] Other drawings were still being worked on at the time of the shipment to bring them to their final form. Probably, as things developed, some of this finishing was done in Mexico City at the Royal Art Academy of San Carlos, with which Suría had a

[31] Sotos, *Los Pintores de la expedición de Alejandro Malaspina* 1 : 129.

[32] A. Valdés to Malaspina, San Lorenzo, October 2, 1790, in Malaspina Correspondencia, 1, MS 278 in MN.

[33] Iris H. W. Engstrand, *Spanish Scientists in the New World,* (Seattle, 1981), p. 103.

lifelong relationship, and with which Cardero had a brief association in 1792–93.

During 1792, Cardero revisited Nootka and California with the *Sutil* and *Mexicana*. His superiors wrote to the viceroy of his participation in the circumnavigation of Vancouver Island. The letter, signed by Alcalá Galiano and Valdés but in the unmistakable handwriting of Cardero, commended the artist in laudatory terms:

> This individual has worked with complete satisfaction and care, as his drawings will prove to Your Excellency. In addition, the detachment of the second pilot, Juan Carrasco, made it so that there fell to the aforementioned Cardero not only the work of drawing maps, a skill that Carrasco lacked, but also all of the duties of the position of second pilot. Cardero went out on all the small boat excursions, which, considering his diminutiveness and lack of strength, were carried out with all the risk and discomfort that you can imagine.

Cardero was singled out as the only person who "helped not only in the drawing but also in copying the papers of the commission."[34]

Cardero's final stay in Mexico began when the *Sutil* and *Mexicana* made port at San Blas on November 22, 1792. He was still being paid the 60 pesos a month that he had been assigned, and his salary continued thus until his arrival in Mexico City, at which time he was reduced to 40 pesos monthly until the termination of his work there. He also was given 270 pesos as an allowance for "his good services" and as repayment for traveling expenses incurred on his overland journey from San Blas to the capital.[35]

An interesting aspect of those salary negotiations, and of the other considerable official correspondence initiated on behalf of Cardero, is that the letters are all in the handwriting of the interested party, with the officers or officer merely signing off at the end

---

[34] Alcalá Galiano and C. Valdés to Revilla Gigedo, México, March 4, 1793, in AGN, Marina 82.

[35] Revilla Gigedo to Alcalá Galiano and C. Valdés, México, March 18, 1793, in Malaspina Pintores, 1788–1795, MS 1827 in MN.

Modo de Pelear de los Indios de Californias, by José Cardero. Museo Naval, Madrid.

of the letters. Clearly Cardero knew what was going on. Perhaps he even initiated the letters, and certainly he was in a position to place things in their most favorable light before the final signatures were affixed.

Once established in the capital, Pepe Cardero was in contact with the Royal Art Academy of San Carlos. Whether as part of his official duties or by choice, the young Andalusian artist drew while in Mexico several items not connected with either his 1791 or 1792 trips to northern waters. One of these was of the Plaza Mayor, the Zócalo of Mexico City.

Cardero returned to Spain accompanying Cayetano Valdés first overland to Veracruz, then on a voyage to Havana, and then back to Spain on the *Cazador.* When, on his arrival there, Valdés wrote to the minister of the navy concerning an illness he had, the letter was in the handwriting of the ever-present Cardero.[36] At a considerably later date the artist was recompensed one hundred *pesos fuertes* for the overland portion of his trip from Mexico City to Veracruz.

[36] C. Valdés to Duque de Alcudia, Cádiz, June 19, 1793, in AHN, Estado 4287. Also C. Valdés to A. Valdés, Aranjuez, February 7, 1794, in Malaspina Pintores, 1788–1795, MS 1827 in MN.

The eventual arrival in Spain of the reports and maps of the voyage of the *Sutil* and *Mexicana* was of considerable importance to the diplomatic solution of the still-pending Nootka Sound Affair with England. A curious aspect of concern about these reports was that the author of the "Relación" is never mentioned, nor is there ever the slightest indication that a considerable series of on-the-spot drawings had been done by Cardero to illustrate the landscape and various events associated with the circumnavigation of Vancouver Island. It is not certain whether Cardero's drawings, either rough sketches or the finished products, arrived with the original report, or whether they were still in the artist's possession.

Once back in Spain, Cardero was assigned to the Naval Department of Cartagena and placed under the orders of Valdés, who was now the commanding officer of the warship *San Fulgencio*.[37] There is no record of what his duties were, but his regular salary was forty escudos a month, plus an overage of another twenty escudos. Later reports indicate that the *San Fulgencio* was engaged in a series of corsair cruises in the Mediterranean, as well as a cruise to support an operation off Toulon. The assignment extended from February until October 1794.

At that time, writing from Madrid, Malaspina expressed his opinion that Cardero should be added to the group that was working at the capital under the expedition's former chief of charts and maps, Felipe Bauzá. This group was putting in order the results of the entire Malaspina expedition preparatory to publication.[38] Just which things Cardero worked on during this stay in Madrid is not fully clear, but it is probable that he divided his time between preparation of the results of both the parent expedition and of the spin-off from it undertaken in the *Sutil* and *Mexicana*. Whatever the case, Cardero was not so fully occupied that he was prevented from asking for temporary transfer to Cádiz in order to be with his family, which clearly by then was established in that coastal naval port.

[37] Order to Miguel Gaston, Aranjuez, February 11, 1794, in Malaspina Pintores, 1788–1795, MS 1827 in MN.

[38] Malaspina to Valdés, October 7, 1794, in Malaspina Expedición Pintores, 1789–1798, MS 2219 in MN.

The upshot of Cardero's request was that Malaspina wrote to the naval minister, Antonio Valdés y Bazán, indicating that Cardero was no longer needed on the scene in Madrid. [39] It was at that point that fortune smiled greatly on Pepe, for he was given a commission in the Spanish Navy at the advanced rank of *contador de navío,* which was equivalent to a senior-grade lieutenant in the line save that he was destined for the supply corps. [40]

There is reason to believe that the sudden appointment of young José Cardero to a substantial rank in the supply corps was not viewed with favor by the local bureaucracy of the Cádiz Naval Department. The appointment resulted from special royal favor rather than prior service in that specialty. In addition, Cardero had no formal naval training, nor any practical experience in supply and accounting. His arrival hardly could have been well received. But if Cardero felt any inadequacy, he must have kept it a secret. King Carlos IV had issued a royal order from the palace at Aranjuez on May 29, 1795, based on the merits Cardero had achieved "during the expedition destined for the exploration of the Strait of Juan de Fuca." The Spanish sovereign had completed the process begun four years earlier at Guayaquil: Cardero was now "an officer and a gentleman" with all the rights, powers, exemptions, and responsibilities thereunto, including a salary that was many times greater than he was receiving when his artistic talent was first recognized while along the South American coast.

Cardero was not even in full possession of his new sinecure when he penned the first of several surviving petitions from which most of the biographical information concerning his new life is known. [41]

[39] Malaspina to A. Valdés, May 24, 1795, in Malaspina Pintores, 1788–1795, MS 1827 in MN.

[40] The actual document was dated at Aranjuez, May 29, 1795, and entitled "Nombramiento de Contador de Navío de la Real Armada para d. Josef Cardero" in AMAB.

[41] Almost all of the post-1795 information concerning José Cardero, except as otherwise noted, is found in the Archivo-Museo Don Alvaro de Bazán at El Viso del Marqués in the section Ministerio de la Marina—Asuntos Personales. The Cardero file contains 16 pages dating from 1795 to 1810. Some of the documents are in Cardero's handwriting and bear his signature and rubric. Others concern him specifically.

This specific petition concerned belated payment of salary and allowances, both subsistence and travel, for the time spent in Madrid under Malaspina's orders. Cardero's propensity for involved and sometimes outlandish petitions was perhaps learned in his long association with the naval customs of the day, or possibly it was almost an innate characteristic.

Cardero's career after his association with the scientific explorations gives no indication that the little Andalusian ever again engaged in any artistic endeavor. Almost all of his art was done while he was with the Malaspina expeditions except for his brief time at San Carlos Academy in Mexico City and the few months he spent under the orders of Malaspina in 1794–95. During both of those periods Cardero's efforts involved completion of drawings begun in 1791 and 1792. There is no mention of any new subjects, though he did make and sign a copy of one of Atanasio Echeverría's drawings resulting from Bodega's Expedition of the Limits to the North of California in 1792. He also did the unsigned view of the Zócalo as earlier indicated.

The brief time when Cardero was once again associated with Malaspina, before the commodore's unanticipated trial and imprisonment, permits clarification of one point, specifically, why at various places in MS 1060 in the Museo Naval collection there are minor corrections in the easily identified handwriting of Malaspina. The commodore lightly copy-edited the account of the voyage of the *Sutil* and *Mexicana* on the version written by Cardero. This reading by Malaspina made it possible for him to include in the huge work that he was preparing some information that postdated his 1791 visit to the Pacific Northwest and California. This final association with Malaspina might have provided an additional motive for Cardero's appointment to officer status except that the royal commission specifically stated that it was the result of the artist's work on the voyage of the *Sutil* and *Mexicana,* with nothing said of his earlier work aboard the *Descubierta* or the *Atrevida.*

Inasmuch as it is probable that José Cardero was never again employed as an artist, but rather became increasingly associated with supply and accounting, he qualifies as the protoartist of the

Pacific Coast. He was not only the most-prolific early artist, he was also quite versatile in that he did general views, native types, and zoological illustrations, and depicted the details of native culture. Cardero's dedication to the Pacific Coast from Guayaquil, Ecuador, to Yakutat Bay, in Alaska, gives his artistic activities the added distinction of a wide geographical range. There are only two drawings known to be by him that are not illustrative of that long coast. One is his view of the Zócalo. The other is an unsigned initial effort; the exact circumstances of its composition by Cardero are as yet unknown, but it was done in September 1789 when a mapping detachment left Montevideo to explore the northeastern coast of the estuary of the Rio de la Plata in modern-day Uruguay. It is a poorly executed view of the Colonia de Sacramento area,[42] which had been recently captured from the Portuguese by the Spaniards. It is obviously a primitive effort, devoid of great merit. It does, however, attest that Cardero had tried his hand earlier and that he did not emerge all of a sudden as an artist when the expedition became short of artistic talent early in 1791.

With the artistic part of his life behind him, by August 17, 1795, Cardero was on station in Cádiz in his new and certainly unfamiliar role. His date of commission made him the junior officer of his rank, but he continually sought promotion and in so doing left behind a considerable record of his activities. Unfortunately, there is no extant single service sheet of his career as an officer, and we are deprived of certain specific bits of information. We do have notice that at age thirty, in a letter written from Cádiz, Cardero asked official permission to marry Gregoria Rosalia de la Vega, a local resident.[43] She was nineteen at the time (January 1798), the daughter of Alonso Antonio de la Vega and María de Terán, both natives of the Isla de León near Cádiz. Such official permission was a necessary step if a service wife ever expected to be eligible for a pension upon the death of her officer husband.

[42] Unsigned, but clearly in Cardero's hand, the view is entitled "Vista de Colonia del Sacramento a distancia como de 1½ millas al rumbo S 85° E." It is reproduced in Sotos, *Los Pintores de la expedición de Alejandro Malaspina,* 2, fig. 26.

[43] Expediente Matrimonial de José Cardero in Archivo General Militar, Segovia.

The marital union was highly productive despite occasional extended absences of José on various naval assignments. Exact enumeration of their progeny is not possible, but a petition on behalf of his sons, Cayetano and José, Jr., written on November 4, 1806, indicated that they were the eldest of five living children. A later petition stated that Cardero and his wife had seven children, presumably living at that time, though there was no indication of how many others might not have survived.

During Cardero's more than twenty years of duty in the navy, mostly in the Naval Department of Cádiz, he served in various capacities both ashore and afloat. He was recipient of occasional promotions, though not without some protests; his advancement was received possibly by his own intervention. From his several petitions, spread over a number of years, we form a one-sided picture of Cardero's activity; however, from some administrative comments added to his surviving petitions, the negative side of his career emerges.

In all his requests for advancement Cardero presented his service with Malaspina and the *Sutil* and *Mexicana* as the first of his merits. Nor is there ever any negative comment about such service except for a marginal note that he had many years ago been fully rewarded for those early activities and that therefore they should have no bearing on later requests for advancement. The most telling of the later negative comments was that, though he had fulfilled his supply-corps duties, he had done nothing that was not commonly done by other officers of the same rank and status. Unfortunately, even when his service with Malaspina and with Valdés and Alcalá Galiano is mentioned, it is never made specific just what those services were, whether artistic, cartographic, journalistic, nautical, secretarial, or menial.

Unlike other companions of the 1792 expedition, Cardero was never in a position to originate official correspondence, save for personal matters, with the result that documentation concerning him is much more fugitive in nature. Valdés, Alcalá Galiano, Vernacci, and Salamanca all had command positions and were therefore required to keep journals, to initiate correspondence, and to make occasional reports. With Pepe Cardero all is not lost, however, particularly because of his unique penmanship and his continuing service as an amanuensis on various occasions, which have permitted the researcher to follow his dim trail.

In what his local supervisors in Cádiz considered the epitome of impropriety, Cardero sought special favors for his two eldest sons. In a petition made directly to the prime minister, Manuel Godoy, the Prince of the Peace, the former artist asked for appointments as *oficiales quintos de ministerio* for his young sons Cayetano and José, Jr. The ridiculousness of such an appointment of children well under the age of ten was self-evident then as well as now, and the request placed Cardero in a poor light with his superiors up the chain of command. In order to facilitate such appointments as he sought, Cardero offered to turn over to the Royal Treasury certain money that he had never yet been paid, as well as some future payments, all of which he thought were due him. He alleged that under wartime conditions and as the result of having a large family, his wife and children were reduced to indigence. Cardero also asserted that, in what he considered similar circumstances, several colleagues had obtained appointments for their children.

The response to Cardero's petition was a rotund no, including a written comment on his reprehensible conduct, not so much for having tried to promote the welfare of his offspring of tender years, but for having sent the petition directly to the prime minister over the heads of his superiors and expressly against their orders. The most important aspect of the petition was Cardero's mention of his own merits as a factor creating his children's eligibility. Of course, he mentioned "the round-the-world expedition of the corvettes [*Descubierta* and *Atrevida*]," making certain not to mention the name of Malaspina, especially in a letter to Godoy, who had been the chief cause of Malaspina's downfall and imprisonment. Cardero did mention the special commission of discovery in the Strait of Juan de Fuca and his subsequent service on the warship *San Fulgencio* in 1794.

Piecing together scraps of information from this petition and other sources, we learn that Cardero was at the main accounting office in the Naval Department of Cádiz with collateral duties at the nearby arsenal of La Carraca from the date of his assignment in 1795 until 1797. He was next sent to the warship *Pelayo,* aboard which, in addition to his regular duties, he carried out special assignments given to him by the commandant general of the Atlantic Squadron. He was involved in the campaigns carried out by that squadron until its arrival at the French port of Brest. There, where the combined French, Dutch, and Spanish fleets were brought together to stage for a planned attack on the British Isles, an operation that never reached fulfillment, Cardero carried out other duties of "the greatest importance" to "the satisfaction of his superiors." He was in that northwestern coastal port of France for two and one-half years, near the end of which he was proposed for promotion to the next highest rank, a recommendation that did not have immediate effect. Among his duties, Cardero served as a scribe, as attested by documents from the Brest campaign that are in his handwriting.

In 1802, Cardero returned to his duties at Cádiz, but was soon sent out again, this time aboard the warship *Argonauta,* part of the previously mentioned squadron sent to the Italian peninsula to pick up some of the royal entourage who were headed for Spain and the gala wedding of Princess María Antonia and the future Fernando VII. Whether or not Cardero played any part in the operation is unknown, save for his presence, but at its conclusion his vessel was sent for decommissioning at the Mediterranean port city of Cartagena, from which point he was transferred back to Cádiz once more.

Cardero returned to his familiar duties, where by dint of seniority on October 26, 1803, he was reclassified as *oficial segundo.* Subsequently, in November 1806, he claimed that he had never been promoted during his active duty at Cádiz or elsewhere. He did have pending at that later date a previous promotion petition of January 1806, which was as yet unanswered or which had been unheeded.

On July 10, 1810, Cardero initiated another petition for promotion to the post of *comisario de guerra,* a request that found very little favor with his immediate superiors, as is obvious from a negative letter of theirs dated July 26, 1810, which resulted in a denial of Cardero's pretensions. The two letters add to our biographical sketch of Cardero by filling in some details since his earlier petitions and by clarifying other activities. These include his participation in operations against Toulon on the Mediterranean coast of France and the actions of a squadron sent to Leghorn (Livorno) in Italy. In the same petition he also mentioned his service in the main accounting office and the arsenals, and concluded it with his new duty as comptroller of the royal gun factory in Cádiz, a position that he had held since establishment of that facility.

According to his detractors, Cardero had served as he had indicated from the time of his promotion to *oficial segundo* until December 29, 1809, but he had in no way distinguished himself above others of his rank. Despite his average performance, he had been promoted on April 29, 1809, to *oficial primero* over the heads of thirteen other more-senior *oficiales segundos*. Though it is nowhere so stated, this advancement may well have been as a result of his reassignment on December 29, 1808, to serve under the orders of the Marqués de Villel, a voting member of the Junta Central of Cádiz, which was the ruling body of the unoccupied area of Spain during the Napoleonic invasion.

In addition to what his associates and superiors thought to have been unwarranted promotions, on October 7, 1809, Cardero had been named comptroller of the gun factory at a substantial salary. They felt that it would be a great injustice to again promote him over men who, besides having greater aptitude and talent, were in all other regards superior. It would have been hard to draft a less favorable opinion of Cardero's case for advancement, and it was forthwith denied.

Hardly was the ink dry on the denial of promotion than a royal order to the contrary was issued: "In the name of King Don Fernando VII, the Council of Spain and the Indies has been pleased to name Don Josef Cardero, *oficial primero* of the Ministry of the Navy and comptroller of accounts of the Royal Gun Factory established here, as Comisario de Guerra. . . ."[44]—signed at Cádiz, July 28, 1810. According to a marginal note on the document, this promotion to *comisario de guerra* resulted in the removal of Cardero's name from the navy rolls.

There is no record of Cardero's subsequent service in army or nonmilitary sources, nor is there any record of the date of his death. It may be supposed that he was still associated with his former commanding officer, Cayetano Valdés, whose important position with the same Council of the Regency could have made the previous appointment possible, though there is no evidence of any intervention.

The hectic period involving much European warfare, the beginnings of the Hispanic-American wars for independence, and the instability of the Spanish government, seems to have obliterated Cardero. Although the Archivo General Militar in Segovia does have a sketchy service record for one of Cardero's sons, it sheds no further light on the last years of that notable early contributor to the historical record of the Pacific Coast.

The Crews

As is frequently the case during the colonial period, the personalities and even the names of individual crew members of the *Sutil* and *Mexicana* are largely unknown. The enlisted men were worthy of greater remembrance, for even the journalist concluded the expedition account with a commendation of their subordination and perseverance during such dangerous and laborious navigation as being worthy of the greatest praise.

Though the journal is completely silent concerning names other than those of the four commissioned officers, supplementary documentation permits us to establish some names, and even some background details in one isolated case. This exception is Boatswain's Mate Pedro Ramos, who was characterized as a veteran of service both at Nootka and along the California coast. Ramos was at Nootka in 1791 when the corvettes *Descubierta* and *Atrevida*

---

[44] The original of the royal order does not appear, but rather a quotation from it that is contained within a letter.

under Alejandro Malaspina made a late summer stop there. His services as a knowledgeable though untrained pilot, whose help would be useful to the scientific exploring expedition, were offered to facilitate its visit to the as-yet-unvisited California coast. Ramos's capacity was soon open to question despite his experience and the high recommendation that he had received from the commanding officer of the Spanish frigate *Concepción,* Ramón Saavedra.[45] Ramos was touted as having twenty-one years of service along the coast, which would place him among the earliest visitors shortly after the founding of the province. Ramos was reported to have visited San Francisco on two occasions six or seven years before 1791.

While with Malaspina, the makeshift pilot proved to be of no value except to recognize that the *Descubierta* and *Atrevida* had missed the port of Monterey and to assure the naval scientists that their precarious position was "satisfactory." This obvious contradiction of reality brought forth Malaspina's rhetorical question: "And who without practical knowledge of these places, without very exact information about them, without a chart worthy of trust, etc., would have contradicted the opinion of a man who had been to Monterey fourteen times, and who spoke with the appearance of truth?"[46]

Subsequent attempts to make port at Monterey in 1791 brought forth an even less flattering evaluation of Ramos and his seamanship: "A very dark day and night, a contrary wind, a chart according to which we were frequently navigating on land, and a pilot full of ignorance and audacity—these were our resources for entering that anchorage." The loss of three anchors in the harbor-entry efforts added to this frustration.[47]

Notwithstanding such demonstrated incompetence, Pedro Ramos was assigned to the 1792 expedition in the more-appropriate capacity of boatswain's mate second-class. Joining Ramos on the northern reconnaissance were José Casimiro Rodríguez, likewise a

[45] Cutter, *Malaspina in California,* pp. 25–26.

[46] Viage en Limpio, MS 181 in MN, and Cutter, *Malaspina in California,* p. 27.

[47] Viage en Limpio, MS 181 in MN, and Cutter, *Malaspina in California,* p. 28.

boatswain's mate second-class, and coxswains Francisco Molina and Lucas Mas. Apparently all served well. Several months after conclusion of the 1792 voyage, writing from Mexico City to Viceroy Revilla Gigedo, Commanders Alcalá Galiano and Valdés recommended all four of their former petty officers as having served during the recently concluded campaign with "such conscientiousness, intelligence, and good conduct" that they were deserving of promotion to the next highest rating.[48]

In addition to the formerly inept pilot, really a boatswain's mate, and his three known companions, the composition of the crews of the *Sutil* and *Mexicana* was a mixture of local mariners, probably from both San Blas and Acapulco, and ten crew members earlier detached by Malaspina from aboard his corvette prior to its December departure for further operations in the Pacific Ocean.[49] We know only four other crew members by name. Two were the bloodletters: Luis Gálvez, on the *Sutil,* and Antonio Durán, on the *Mexicana.* The other two were Artillerymen José Cavo and Manuel González, both of whom had enlisted in Cádiz in 1789.

Later, at Nootka, while making last-minute preparations for the impending circumnavigation of Vancouver Island, nine more men were assigned aboard. Five joined the ranks of the *Sutil:* two marines, one artilleryman, one caulker, and a seaman. The latter was a replacement for an original crew member who had become ill. The *Mexicana*'s crew was strengthened by the addition of a carpenter and of three soldiers from the Catalonian Volunteer Company stationed at Nootka.[50] Though those figures may be subject to minor error, the total operating complement of the *Sutil* stood at twenty-three, while its sister ship had twenty-four. A document of later date states with some certainty that there were precisely twenty-five aboard each vessel, including officers and

[48] Alcalá Galiano and C. Valdés to Revilla Gigedo, México, March 4, 1793, in AGN, Marina 92.

[49] Novo y Colson, ed., *Viaje político-científico alrededor del mundo por las corbetas Descubierta y Atrevida . . . ,* pp. 205–6.

[50] Lionel Cecil Jane, ed., *A Spanish Voyage to Vancouver and the Northwest Coast of America* (London, 1930), p. 16, does not specify that the latter were Catalonian Volunteers.

men. It is not known whether on their return to Nootka after the summer of exploration all nine or any of the late reinforcements were returned to their previous duty stations.

In view of the prior services of the combined crews, it is possible to say that all persons associated with the exploration in the summer of 1792 had been to California previously except Dionisio Alcalá Galiano, who in 1791 had been attending to duties in Central Mexico. Those who had visited previously had come either as a part of Malaspina's group or with the San Blas vessels that regularly ran the coast in supplying the missions and presidios of the new province, or as part of the exploration force sent by Spain to the British Columbia and Alaska coast.

The Californians

The visit of the *Sutil* and *Mexicana* is an interesting event in colonial California history showing the area and its people from a different perspective than that from which they are portrayed in internally generated documentation of the same period. The significant Californians included José Dario Argüello, military commandant of Monterey Presidio and acting governor; Father Fermín Francisco de Lasuén, prelate of the Franciscan missions with his headquarters at San Carlos (also called Carmel both then and now); and Fathers Pascual Martínez de Arenaza and José Francisco de Paula Señán, who were the priests assigned to that mission at the time of the 1792 visit. These were the three Franciscans depicted in Cardero's drawing of the convent, church, and rancherias of Mission Carmel done in 1791, since there had been no clerical personnel changes in the interval. No other names of California residents are specified in the account, but the supporting cast included 202 men, women, and children at Monterey, the three non-Indian, non-Franciscan residents of San Carlos Mission, and most of the 770 natives congregated at that mission on the banks of the Carmel River. Most of the natives were either Rumsen or Esselen Indians, who became a source of anthropological interest to the visitors of 1792.

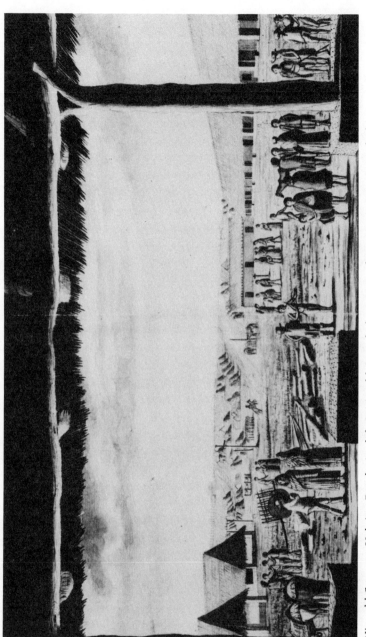

Vista del Convento, Yglecia y Rancherias de la Misión del Carmelo, by José Cardero. Museo Naval, Madrid.

José Argüello[51] was born in Querétaro about 1753 and enlisted in the dragoons as a private in 1773. Before coming to California, he had served in the ranks in Sonora, an area of frequent Indian conflict. Following promotion to ensign in 1781, Argüello came to California on the Rivera expedition of that year, narrowly escaping the Yuma Massacre, which cost the lives of many of his companions. He subsequently served consecutively at San Gabriel and Santa Barbara, and as commandant of San Francisco until March 1791. He served as commandant of Monterey Presidio from 1791 to 1796.

Argüello was well liked because he was very supportive of the priests in their missionary endeavor, so much so that many considered him a *frailero,* a somewhat derogatory term for those who were highly partial to the spiritual aspect of the conquest. He later served again in San Francisco and in Santa Barbara. In 1815 he was promoted to the governorship of Lower California, which had been separated from Upper California. The Wars for Independence in Mexico resulted in his transfer to Guadalajara, where he retired. His death in relative poverty occurred in 1827.

Argüello was reported to be of pure Spanish stock, and his wife as well. Their progeny included a priest, José Ignacio Máximo Argüello, and three other sons, Gervasio, Santiago, and Luis. The latter became governor of Upper California during the Mexican period. The long vigil of a daughter, María de la Concepción (Concha), for her departed noble Russian suitor, Nicolai Rezanof, was inventively immortalized in a once-popular romantic poem, *Concepcion de Arguello,* by Bret Harte.

San Carlos Mission had two regularly assigned priests. Father Pascual Martínez de Arenaza,[52] like his prelate, Lasuén, was from the Spanish province of Alava. He arrived in Mexico in 1785 and went from there to California about two years later. Arenaza, as he was called rather than Martínez, had but one regular mission assignment during his decade of California ministry—San Carlos.

[51] Bancroft, *History of California* 2:358–61.

[52] Maynard Geiger, *Franciscan Missionaries in Hispanic California, 1769–1848* (San Marino, 1969), p. 154.

He suffered from ill health, made little impact in the Franciscan work, returned to the home college of San Fernando in Mexico City in 1797, and died there of tuberculosis some two years later. Also at San Carlos to inform and entertain the visiting scientists was a then-youthful José Francisco de Paula Señán. Born in Barcelona, he was a vigorous thirty-two years of age and had been a Franciscan since 1774 and a resident in America since 1784. Señán came to California at about the same time as his fellow Franciscan Arenaza. Though he was an excellent missionary, he suffered from burnout after ten years and returned to Mexico City in 1795. At the home college, at the request of the new viceroy, Marqués de Branciforte, he compiled a report on the reasons why the colonization of California was progressing so slowly. Two years later Señán returned to California and took up residence at Mission San Buenaventura, the mission with which his name has become so closely associated as a result of his twenty-seven years of service there. A man of "zeal, prudence, virtue, and knowledge," in 1812 he became the fourth father president of the California mission chain. In August 1823 he died at age sixty-three, having seen the curtain ring down on Spanish colonial control of California a year earlier, when he and others took the oath of allegiance to the Mexican independent regency of Agustín Iturbide.[53]

Most important among the local residents, as far as the visitors were concerned, was the gentlemanly, urbane, and helpful prelate of the Franciscans, Father Lasuén. Except for the founding father president, the well-known and recently canonized Junípero Serra, there are few persons more frequently mentioned in the history of the region. Any earlier lack of recognition of the affable Basque leader has been compensated for in recent years by publication of his collected writings[54] and by an excellent biographical study of his life.[55] Those two works have dispelled any doubts and myths associated with a notable missionary career. Even as far away as Lasuén's native city of Vitoria, capital of the Basque province of

[53] Geiger, *Franciscan Missionaries in Hispanic California*, pp. 235–39.
[54] Kenneally, trans. and ed., *The Writings of Fermín Francisco de Lasuén*.
[55] Guest, *Fermín Francisco de Lasuén (1736–1802): A Biography*.

Alava, there is a Lasuén society dedicated to promulgation of historical information concerning a worthy figure who was born and had most of his religious formation there.

Lasuén, second great prelate of Spanish California, has often been compared with his predecessor, Serra. This is hard to do and is probably counterproductive. Each was a man for his times. Serra's time was that of first beginnings, and he was responsible for the founding of nine of the already-prospering eleven missions that Malaspina learned of during his visit of 1791. Lasuén, by temperament and personality, was a developer and administrator, and in turn he became responsible for the next nine missions, of which two had been founded before Malaspina arrived in 1791 and two others were being founded at the time of the visit of the *Descubierta* and *Atrevida*. When the schooners *Sutil* and *Mexicana* arrived a year later in 1792, the mission system had thirteen of its eventual twenty-one units.

It is not Lasuén's significance compared to Serra that is important at this point, but rather his ability and willingness to help the official visitors who were on the king's business in their scientific studies. Lasuén's view of his responsibility to both majesties—to God and king—would bring forth nothing short of his best efforts. On both occasions he was attentive to every detail. In September 1791 at the time of arrival of Malaspina's corvettes, Lasuén was absent from San Carlos, but he dropped everything to hurry back to assist Malaspina in every way possible. Lasuén's usefulness led the expedition leader to state that

> from the moment of his arrival so great was his activity for our collections of natural history, so prolific and detailed his information and reflections on the prosperity of these missions, and finally so affable, natural, and religiously abundant was his hospitality at any hour that either the officers or the persons of other subaltern classes visited him at the mission, that he would be poorly described in any other way than that of perpetual recognition and appreciation.[56]

[56]Cutter, *Malaspina in California*, p. 31.

Both groups of explorers felt fortunate in having the father president as an informed source. The 1792 visitors could only second what had been said earlier by the commander of the *Atrevida,* José Bustamante, concerning Lasuén's hospitality, which was of such magnitude that it was impossible to forget "without being ungrateful for such splendid and attentive conduct." [57]

Lasuén was a devoted and experienced priest. Born in June 1736, he became a Franciscan at the age of fifteen. In 1761 he arrived in Mexico after volunteering for the American mission field. As a young priest he labored in the Sierra Gorda missions, an area of service of the College of San Fernando de Mexico. Under Junípero Serra, Lasuén went to the Lower California missions when the Franciscans replaced the expelled Jesuits. In the northern mission of San Francisco de Borja, Lasuén served with notable success until 1773, when he was transferred to Upper California. Though he visited at various missions, most of Lasuén's early California years (1775–85) were spent at the southernmost establishment, San Diego. Generally discontent in California, he nonetheless became successor to Serra. For eighteen years, including the dates of both visits of the Spanish naval explorers, he was prelate, maintaining headquarters at San Carlos. His premature greyness, belying his not-too-advanced years, gave rise to a legend concerning his age, a source of comment by some visitors. By 1803, when Lasuén died, the missions had been stabilized. He is credited with building them economically and architecturally, particularly the nine founded during his presidency.

Lasuén was a man of personal charm and hospitality, but he was also a good businessman and a convincing advocate for California. The Rumsen and Esselen word lists and the accompanying catechism obtained by Alcalá Galiano and Valdés had been made at the request of the "captain of the frigate *Gertrudis,*" Alonso Torres-Guerra. [58] Possibly the person making the request was Juan de la

---

[57] Bustamante, Viaje de las Corbetas Descubierta y Atrevida . . . , MS 13 in Archivo del Ministerio de Asuntos Exteriores (AMAE), Madrid. Cutter, *Malaspina in California,* p. 31.

[58] Journal entry, Vargas Ponce, MS 1060, f. 84.

Bodega y Quadra, since after his arrival on October 10 aboard the *Activa,* Bodega was senior officer and therefore by naval protocol was in command of all vessels in the area. Logically, because of the nature of his appointment and his long association with the Mexico-based natural scientist José Mariano Moziño, Bodega should have had much greater interest than the recently arrived Captain Torres, nominal commanding officer of the war frigate. Had the word list and the catechism been the work of any other priest, Lasuén would have so indicated. Together these two documents are testimony of Franciscan attempts to explain Christianity to the Indians in their native languages—an effort not often appreciated by opponents of the Spanish Catholic missionary program.

A signal service only recently appreciated was Lasuén's other anthropological interest. In 1791 he sent word post haste to the Santa Barbara Channel missions that the local priests should forward without delay examples of local Indian handiwork. The result of his request was what is now a unique collection of the earliest known northern Chumash basketry,[59] preserved in fine condition today in the Museo de América of Madrid, the principal repository of artifacts gathered on Malaspina's five-year cruise.

About the time of Malaspina's departure in 1791, Lasuén wrote a flowery letter of thanks to Malaspina and his cocommander, Bustamante. There is no equivalent letter for the 1792 visit, yet no incident occurred to make the sentiments then any different than at the earlier time when Lasuén had said:

> We have seen that you, with your respective officers and crews, strive to satisfy the will of our sovereign and the glory of our nation alone. May God bless you and grant you perseverance, for that demonstrated by the two Spanish corvettes here in this port assures us that the expedition should be more glorious, more useful and beneficial to all human society, and of more honor to the nation than all the others of this type.
>
> You, your officers, and seamen have comported yourselves here among Christians and gentiles in such a way as must certainly

[59] Donald C. Cutter, "The Return of Malaspina," *The American West,* 15, no. 1 (January–February 1978), p. 17.

contribute to the same spiritual and temporal progress as your graces desire.' . . .[60]

This had been in response to Malaspina's letter, which briefly summarized the nature of the father president's contributions as follows:

> Your Paternal Reverence has contributed considerably to the increase of our collections for natural history with various contributions of great value, has sent out his neophytes hunting and fishing, and has conveyed to us all the information that we can use for forming a thorough knowledge concerning this country.[61]

Just as Malaspina had left delighted with Lasuén's contribution, the *Sutil* and *Mexicana* crews could have been no less so. Though the 1792 visit was twice as long as Malaspina's, it certainly did not place the same strain on local resources as the visit of the *Descubierta* and *Atrevida,* which had carried nearly four times as many people aboard. Among Lasuén's significant contributions in 1792 was what stands as the most-extensive information concerning the Esselen and Rumsen Indians, groups that early became culturally extinct, thereby making Lasuén's contribution unique.

Other Visitors

Among those who happened to be present while the *Sutil* and *Mexicana* made their California visit of 1792 were the two Spanish naval captains Juan Francisco de la Bodega y Quadra and Alonso Torres-Guerra, commander of the *Gertrudis,* a royal frigate recently assigned to the Pacific area. The former was a veteran captain at the peak of a notable career. He was senior naval officer in the area and had frequently carried out collateral duty as commander of the naval base and shipyard at San Blas. In contrast, Torres was a very junior four-striper, with the gold braid of his latest stripe not yet

---

[60] Lasuén to Malaspina and Bustamante, San Carlos de Monterey, September 23, 1791, in Malaspina Correspondencia, 2, MS 279 in MN. Translated in Cutter, *Malaspina in California,* p. 36.

[61] Malaspina to Lasuén, Port of Monterey, September 21, 1791, in Apuntes, noticias y correspondencia pertenecientes a la espedición de Malaspina, MS 427 in MN. Translated in Cutter, *Malaspina in California,* p. 36.

darkened by the effects of salt air. Torres was uncomfortable in his first major command, so much so that he tried unsuccessfully to retain all the prerogatives of command though he was clearly outranked aboard his own ship when, in Lima, Captain Bodega came aboard for transportation first to San Blas and subsequently to the Northwest Coast, the assignment from which the vessel was returning when it put into Monterey in September 1792. Bodega had gone to Nootka to meet there with his British counterpart, George Vancouver, seeking a solution to the prolonged dispute over sovereignty and rights of trade and transit in what Spain had previously considered as a Spanish lake—the Pacific Ocean. At Nootka, Bodega shifted his person and therefore senior command to the ship *Activa.* Shortly after the arrival of Torres in Monterey, Bodega also put into port aboard the *Activa,* with the result that he became the senior officer present and thus commanded all operations. These were familiar waters to the senior man. He had first navigated them as a young officer when in 1775 he had taken his tiny vessel, the *Sonora,* to 58° north latitude, thereby expanding Spain's northern claims.

Bodega was born in Peru of Spanish parents of Basque ancestry. He became a midshipman, dropped out, and reenlisted. He had a very successful naval career, with most of his duty in the Pacific but also some service in Europe.[62] Both as a mariner and a person, he was held in high esteem by Spaniards and foreigners alike. A consummate gentleman, a bit given to ostentation, he was in many regards the model naval officer. In 1792 he was nearing the end of his interesting career, a biographical study of which has never been adequately done, but is currently being undertaken.[63] As a figure in regional history, his name is well known, and his

[62] A summary of Bodega's early life is in Ordenes Militares, Santiago—Juan de la Bodega y Quadra (Lima, 1776) in AHN. See also Cutter, "California, Training Ground for Spanish Naval Heroes," pp. 115–17.

[63] Bodega's participation in the affairs of 1792 is detailed in his Viage a la Costa NO de la America septentrional, MS 146 in AMAE. Bodega indicated that one of his primary purposes on the Northwest Coast at that time was to support the hydrographic operations of the schooners *Sutil* and *Mexicana.* A long-needed biography of Bodega is nearing completion by Freeman Tovell of Victoria, British Columbia.

activity is still commemorated several places in the geography of the Pacific Coast. Though he seemed in normally good health in October 1792, less than seventeen months later he died in Mexico City.

The other captain present is almost unknown in America and should be better known in Spain than is the case. With the passage of time he became an important officer in the Spanish naval picture, exceeding Bodega's advancement by far. Alonso Torres-Guerra [64] became in his day more important than any of the group of notables present at Monterey in the fall of 1792, with the exception of Cayetano Valdés. Both Torres and Valdés were born on the banks of the Rio Guadalquivir in Sevilla, with Torres about thirteen years senior.

Young Alonso Torres began his naval career as a midshipman at Cádiz in September 1770. Promotions followed in rapid succession: *alférez de fragata* (ensign), 1774; *alférez de navío* (lieutenant, junior grade), 1776; *teniente de fragata* (also, lieutenant, junior grade), 1778; *teniente de navío* (lieutenant, senior grade), 1781; and commander in 1782. His latest promotion was to the rank of captain in 1792. Torres sailed in the Mediterranean, the Atlantic, and the Pacific under the command of great Spanish naval figures, saw action against the British, and received his first minor command, the brigantine *Ardilla* in 1788. His second ship, the frigate *Gertrudis,* carried Torres around the Horn to Peru where its home port was Callao.

It was from Callao that Torres and the *Gertrudis* were ordered to make the voyage to the Pacific Northwest that eventually brought that vessel to Monterey. By that date Torres was midway in a career of importance. He remained in the Pacific until late 1794, when his vessel was ordered back to Spain. The *Gertrudis* formed part of a convoy that coincidentally contained the *Descubierta* and *Atrevida,* likewise homeward bound. The ships were joined together for a safer trip to Cádiz because of war conditions.

Upon arrival in Spain, Torres was granted four months' leave to

[64] All biographical material on Alonso de Torres-García is from Pavia, *Galería Biográfica de los Generales de Marina* 3:583–88.

recuperate his health. Once he was back to active service, his career was filled with command, military action, and honors. He was granted an encomienda in the knighthood Order of Calatrava, from which he obtained a regular income, and he was appointed military commandant of the province of San Lucar de Barrameda at the mouth of the Rio Guadalquivir. In 1808, Torres became a commodore. Two years later he was named as a representative to the then-governing Cortes of Spain, and as a result was a signer of the Spanish Constitution of 1812. By 1815 he was elevated to rear admiral and had been awarded the prestigious Great Cross of San Hermenegildo. His subsequent assignments were as acting major general of the navy, then military governor of Sevilla and, finally, of Cádiz, until his retirement in 1824. Death eventually came to Alonso Torres in 1832 at age seventy-eight while he was living in retirement at Cocentaina in Alicante province.

Several other notable figures were present in the Monterey area in the autumn of 1792. One previously mentioned was Governor Roméu's widow, Josefa Sandoval, who, after awaiting passage to Mexico aboard the *Gertrudis,* actually departed on October 26. Another passenger on that same vessel was a British merchant captain, Matthew Weatherhead, whose story is very interesting.[65] He had been the commanding officer of the merchant vessel *Matilde,* part of a five-unit convoy that left from Spithead, England, destined for Port Jackson in Australia. From there he set out on a whaling expedition in the South Pacific. His vessel became wrecked two hundred leagues from Tahiti while in 22° south latitude, but he and his crew, including his young nephew, "John Brand," had made their way in small boats to Tahiti. There he was picked up by Captain James Baker of the British corvette "Finney" (really the *Jenny*) and taken to Clayoquot on Vancouver Island. Next he went to Nootka with Captain William Brown of the English merchant vessel *Butterworth.* Weatherhead was cited in the 1792 "Relación" as an authority on whaling. Among other things, while at Nootka the shipless captain had served as a witness and

[65] The saga of Matthew Weatherhead is told in outline in Revilla Gigedo to Conde de Aranda, México, January 8, 1793, in AHN, Estado 4290.

signed the bill of sale of the 47-ton *Adventure* to Bodega y Quadra by U.S. merchant captain Robert Gray.[66] In a humanitarian but not totally altruistic move, Weatherhead and his nephew were being returned to England under escort of a Spanish naval officer.

The escorting officer was another passenger on the *Gertrudis*. He was Felix Cepeda, an officer with bilingual capacity whose English had been used in the deliberations between Bodega and Vancouver. He was also the author of a little-known report on the diplomatic situation on the Northwest Coast.[67] He had been given the assignment of returning Weatherhead to England via San Blas, Mexico City, Veracruz, and Cádiz.

Another interesting visitor was the natural scientist quoted in the "Relación," José Mariano Moziño.[68] He was in the process of writing his excellent contemporary account *Noticias de Nutka*. Though, like much of the other writing being produced, it was slow to find publication in any worthwhile outlet, today it is considered a classic description highly regarded by students of local anthropology and history. Moziño had acted as the official botanist of the Expedition of the Limits to the North of California headed by Bodega. A most-versatile scholar, with competence in theology, ethics, medicine, mathematics, and botany, Moziño spent from April 29 to September 21, 1792, at the Spanish establishment at Nootka. He was part of a team that collected species, made observations, and drew representations of Nootka at its zenith. Accompanying Moziño to Nootka and returning with him to Mexico via Monterey was a competent artist, Atanasio Echeverría. The two made great contributions to Pacific Coast history, includ-

[66] The bill of sale that Weatherhead witnessed is in AGN, Marina 73.

[67] On the basis of his stay at Nootka in 1792, Cepeda wrote the extended 204-page treatise "Memoria Histórica de la Costa Norueste de la America Septentrional," a manuscript probably finished about 1795 and containing two nearly equal parts: (1) Memoria de los Viages Europeos en la Costa Norueste de la America Septentrional and (2) Reflexiones sobre el resultado de nuestras expediciones . . . sobre el objeto Político de Nutka.

[68] The story of the Mexican savant is treated in Iris Wilson [Engstrand], ed., *Noticias de Nutka*, and in greater detail in Engstrand, *Spanish Scientists in the New World*.

ing the artist's drawing of the California quail done at Monterey in 1792.

Moziño was particularly enthusiastic concerning the potential of California and of its future. In this he echoed what had been said by the *Sutil* and *Mexicana* group. After his return to Mexico and various duties there, he eventually went to Spain. In Madrid in 1808, Joseph Bonaparte, Napoleon's brother, who had been established as king of Spain, appointed the Mexican scientist as director of the Royal Museum of Natural History and professor of zoology at the Royal Academy of Medicine. The fall of Joseph Bonaparte brought the downfall of Moziño, who was branded as a collaborationist. He was compelled to flee to France, carrying with him his many specimens. After a pathetic series of misadventures, Moziño became a disillusioned man. He finally returned to Spain, where in 1820 he died in Barcelona.

From among this group of notable visitors must have come most of the twenty-one persons that Lasuén had at table on September 25. Except for some of the international dinner parties at Nootka at the height of the Nootka Sound deliberations, this probably rates as the most high-powered assemblage in regional colonial history. Though no list is available, the group must have included most of the following figures: Spanish naval officers Torres-Guerra, Valdés, Alcalá Galiano, Salamanca, and Vernacci; Matthew Weatherhead and his nephew, John Brand; the three Franciscans, Lasuén, Señán, and Arenaza; Josefa Sandoval, the widow of Governor Roméu, and her children; Pérez Hernández, Roméu's adjutant; Argüello and his wife; artists José Cardero and Atanasio Echeverría; Botanist Moziño; Felix Cepeda; and Monterey Company Lieutenant Hermenegildo Sal.

4. Homeward to San Blas

During the 1792 voyage Alcalá Galiano and Valdés performed hydrographic chores assigned to them by higher authority such as their major effort in circumnavigation of Vancouver Island. They also felt an obligation to extend their efforts to clarify matters concerning which there were contemporary doubts. One of these involved their suspicion that the submerged mountain chain, the tops of which form the offshore Channel Islands, was greatly misplaced on the map that had been provided to them on their departure from San Blas and Acapulco. That chart, referred to as the San Blas pilots' map, is reproduced in this study. Superimposed on the basic map are those same islands in the positions determined for them by observations made from aboard the *Sutil* and *Mexicana*. The map, as altered, clearly shows the disparity that the naval scientists earlier suspected.

The entire map is in the hand of the versatile José Cardero. Probably the base map was a copy made by him either at San Blas or later at Monterey. An effort was made to give a three-dimensional quality to the new positions, whereas the San Blas pilots' map conveys an impression of flatness. As regards the erroneous positions assigned by the San Blas pilots, it should be borne in mind that in pilotage school students did not receive the sophisticated cartographic training that Alcalá Galiano and Valdés had obtained both at midshipmen's school and, subsequently, during duty assignments to prominent mapmaking projects both on the

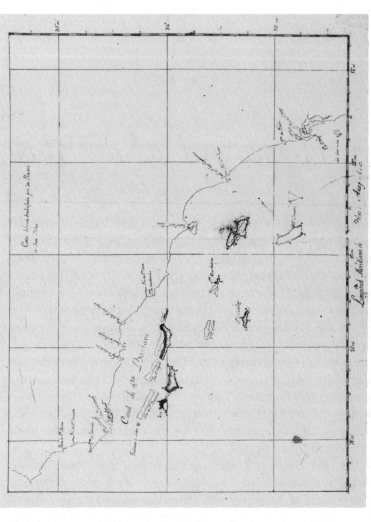

José Cardero's copy of the San Blas pilots' map (*Carta esférica trabajada por los Pilotos de San Blas*). Museo Naval, Madrid.

Iberian Peninsula and overseas. There is no evidence of visits to the Channel Islands by any of the pilots, nor any evidence of efforts to chart them with any degree of perfection. When they were in the Santa Barbara Channel, the pilots sailed by geonavigational techniques, using visual recognition of familiar landmarks such as headlands, peaks, and islands, and guided by the feel of winds and currents, as well as by the color of sea water. There were few if any temptations to establish their position by complicated celestial navigation. Dead reckoning, visual acuity, and previous local experience normally were brought into play. Needless to say, the pilots were not well served by their own maps.

In rectifying the positions of the Channel Islands, the *Mexicana* sailed to the north of them, closer to land, while the *Sutil* kept to the south, outside the protection of the islands. The revised positions on the map were thus the result of two views of the same landforms.[1]

After the attempt to correct the position of the offshore islands of Alta California and after passing the harbor entrance at San Diego, the schooners hugged the Baja California shore until, tiring of the highly routine nature of work concerning areas quite well known, the commanders decided to leave the coast in order to ascertain the exact position of Los Alijos. These potentially dangerous rocks jut up about 180 miles offshore and were thought to be a menace to southbound navigation.

On October 31, 1791, the Acapulco-bound Manila galleon *San Andrés*, Lieutenant Joaquín Marquina commanding, had reported sighting the rocks in 24° 36' north latitude.[2] José Espinosa y Tello, a contemporary naval officer who was quite critical of the *Sutil* and *Mexicana* positions at a later date, on his own authority corrected Marquina's observed position by moving it about ten miles northward. Since Marquina's 1791 observation was at con-

[1] Journal entry, Vargas Ponce, MS 1060, MN, ff. 87v–88v.
[2] Marquinna's sighting is treated in Josef de Espinosa, *Memoria sobre las observaciones astronómicas . . .* (Madrid, 1805).

siderable variance with earlier estimates of position, the *Sutil* and *Mexicana* captains hit on what was considered a foolproof plan to locate the rocky sentinels. They would sail westward on parallel tracks with the *Mexicana* assigned to 24° 56' N and the companion vessel to 24° 30' N. The interval was narrow enough that they might sight anything significant between the latitudes, as well as within a dozen miles either north or south of the two tracks—that being their apparent maximum range of visibility.[3]

Notwithstanding the seemingly adequate plan, an unexpected southward set by wind and currents carried the vessels, despite efforts to the contrary, as much as twenty-five miles southward, with both vessels experiencing the same decrease in latitude. It is no wonder that neither schooner came close to Los Alijos and that they became convinced that Marquina had been wrong in his observation. Owing to the poor navigational characteristics of the small schooners, it was felt unwise and perhaps impossible to attempt to regain their lost latitude. The search for the elusive rocks was abandoned, and they headed for San Blas. On their own *carta esférica,* Alcalá Galiano and Valdés charted the rocks in 25° 10' N.[4] Modern atlases give their latitude as almost exactly 25°, a latitude in which they would have been found by the schooners had they not suffered the unanticipated southward set.

A final chore for the *Sutil* and *Mexicana* involved carrying out earlier orders to examine the well-known offshore islands of central Mexico, the Islas Marías and Isabela.[5] Their geographical position, quite close to San Blas, would seem to have been well established; however, Malaspina's calculations had been at such variance with those of the San Blas pilots that verification of their placement was necessary. The principal Marías Islands—María Madre,

[3] Journal entry, Vargas Ponce, MS 1060, MN, f. 90.

[4] "Carta Esférica de los reconocimientos hechos en la costa N.O. de America en 1791 y 1792 por las Goletas Sutil y Mexicana y otros buques de S.M.," in *Relación del viage hecho por las goletas Sutil y Mexicana en el año de 1792 para reconocer al estrecho de Fuca,* vol. 2 (Madrid, 1802), carta 1. Vol. 2 has its own title of *Atlas para el viage de las goletas Sutil y Mexicana.*

[5] Journal entry, Vargas Ponce, MS 1060, MN, ff. 91–92.

María Magdalena, and María Cleofas—were quickly observed and charted, after which the navigators turned their attention to Isla Isabela. Unsatisfactory late-November weather conditions prevented ideal observation. The prospect of a warm welcome at San Blas, a fitting conclusion of a most difficult mission, prompted the ships' officers to hasten homeward.

In a final summary of the results of the northern mission, the journalist wrote:

> Our crews arrived in perfect health and full of delight at the happy ending of an expedition which was very laborious and full of risk, taking into consideration the kind of vessel employed in it. The purpose for which these ships had been fitted out having been accomplished, we handed them over to the officer commanding the department [of San Blas], and prepared ourselves to return to Spain by way of Mexico [City] and Veracruz.[6]

[6] Engstrand, *Spanish Scientists in the New World*, p. 126.

PART TWO

Translation and Annotation of a Manuscript Account of the Voyage of the Spanish Schooners *Sutil* and *Mexicana* Dealing with Operations from Nootka Sound, Vancouver Island, to San Blas on the Coast of Nayarit from Late August to Late November, 1792

The schooners leave Nootka. The wind carries them away from the coast and they cannot approach it until in 47° {north} latitude. They explore the Entrada de Hezeta¹ and follow the coast until they reach the discoveries made by the corvettes Descubierta *and* Atrevida. *The weather carries them away again, and they do not sight land until Cape Mendocino.² They are unable to carry out exploration until reaching Point Reyes, where they again sight land and anchor in the Port of Monterey.*

August 1792. The onset of good weather and our desire of examining the coast from the Entrance of [Juan de] Fuca to San Blas made us hasten to take our quick departure from Nootka. On the 31st we inspected the bottoms of our schooners, which were found to be without damage, and we smeared them with grease so that we could make our departure that same night, taking advantage of the land breeze.

In fact, at twelve midnight we set sail, after sending to Commander [George] Vancouver a copy of the part of the map of our explorations that he had chosen and having received from him his

¹ Entrada de Hezeta was the name given to the mouth of the Columbia River after it was first discovered on August 17, 1775, by the expedition led by Spanish Lieutenant Bruno de Hezeta.

² Prominent geographical names still in regular use will not be identified, such as Cape Mendocino, Point Reyes, Monterey, and so on.

map of the area lying between the Boca de Pinedo[3] and Cape North,[4] including the adjacent islands, and of the coast from the Entrance of Fuca to 45° latitude. We left under a fresh wind from the north and with a clear sky, but shortly it grew calm and at dawn we had not yet cleared the Punta de Arrecifes.[5]

As the day progressed the favorable appearances of the weather were lost, and during the night a fresh east wind commenced. At sunset we remained within sight of the Nootka coast in 49° 13′ latitude and 21° 34′ longitude west of San Blas.[6]

The wind continued from the E and ESE, forcing us to tack to the south, which separated us from the coast. Since our intention was to run it completely and to map it from the Entrance of Fuca to Monterey, to which we were headed, we hoisted as little sail as possible so as not to move off from the coast, but the heavy wind and sea took us so far off course that, when it began to slacken at noon on [September] 4, we were in 48° 20′ latitude and 21° 54′ longitude, and therefore forty leagues from the coast.

The wind was blowing from the first quadrant, and we hauled the wind in order to sight land in the highest latitude that the wind would permit, but we were unable to do so until dawn of the 7th in 47° latitude. It was so clear that with only the light of dawn its configuration could be well distinguished. In the interior to the SE there was a high mountain with a flat top [Mt. St. Helens], and to the NE a range of mountains [the Cascades] with peaks. Between these the land was flat, and the entire coast has a low beach down to the sea.

But when the sun came out everything was covered with fog, which impeded our view of the land. We approached it with

[3] The Boca de Pinedo was probably Kingcome Inlet in the Queen Charlotte Strait area.

[4] Cape North was a headland on Queen Charlotte Island.

[5] The craggy Punta de Arrecifes was at the south entrance to Nootka Sound, being more frequently called Punta de San Estevan.

[6] "The meridian of San Blas is considered to be 99° 5′ west of Cádiz, and from it are calculated all of the longitudes that follow"—JOURNAL. [This was as close to accurate as possible, a reflection of the use of new methods for determination of longitudes].

leadline in hand until the noise of the surf warned us of its proximity, having arrived at this point at 10:30 A.M. and in a depth of
18 fathoms, with fine, black, sandy bottom. We steered SE ¼S
[157 ½°] and sailed with the same precautions, never ceasing to
hear the noise that the sea made against the beach, and maintaining a depth of 18 fathoms with the same sort of bottom.

The wind had remained light from four o'clock on, coming
from the north and thereabouts, and in these circumstances it blew
softly from the NW. A little after noon it cleared somewhat and we
were able to observe a low point bearing 124°, but the fog returned
so thick that the schooners could not see each other and kept
station by the sound of signal guns. In this situation the wind
shifted to the W and began to freshen, placing us in the critical
position of finding ourselves on a coast without ports, inhabited by
Indians who had given proof of their ferocity by the murder of
seven sailors of the launch of the schooner *Sonora* in the year
1775 [7]—completely surrounded by fog, and in two vessels given
considerably to drifting. We took the precaution of hauling the
wind with as much sail as possible, steering S ¼SW [192 ½°].
Fortunately, the wind slackened at 3:00 P.M., returning to the
NW, and as the sky cleared, land became visible, toward which
we steered immediately. So great was our desire to examine it
that we only yielded to the contrary conditions of the weather,
finding ourselves with very poor means of resisting them. With
other normal vessels we would not have stayed so far away from
it, nor would we have lost latitude, but the poor characteristics
of these schooners obliged us not to endanger ourselves with such
an indiscretion, which was as inexcusable as it probably was
useless.

The land that we sighted was a great bay that lay between Punta

[7] The site of the 1775 incident was named by the Spaniards the Punta de los
Mártires. It is now known as Grenville Bay. Offshore there is a reef bearing the name
of the small vessel *Sonora*, the longboat of which had been attacked by the local
Indians with dire results. The specific site of the attack seems to have been near the
mouth of Quinault River just south of Cape Elizabeth. See Herbert K. Beals, *For
Honor and Country: The Diary of Bruno de Hezeta* (Portland, 1985), p. 77.

Gorda[8] and Punta San Cayetano.[9] In this interval there is a little harbor explored by the American captain [Robert] Gray, one with little water at its entrance, a map of which was given to us by Don Juan de la Bodega [y Quadra]. But night prevented us from exploring it. It was a calm night and we spent it lying to and by tacking so as not to get beyond the Entrada de Hezeta.

At dawn we were on a low coast with a cape to the SE that we guessed was that of San Roque, the northern cape of the entrance seen by Lieutenant Don Bruno de Hezeta on August 17, 1775, and which he called Asumción [sic].[10] This matter was one of the principal ones of our commission, for since that time it had not been explored by the Spaniards, nor had the English in their explorations along this coast seen such an entrance. Captain Vancouver, who had explored it very minutely, said that no considerable entrance could exist along all of it from 45° to the Entrance of [Juan de] Fuca. We desired to combine these and other trustworthy reports, which were in little agreement upon this important point. Therefore we had bound ourselves not to spare any means to carry that out, no matter how risky they might be. Any mariner— who is aware that a fresh wind, in which normal vessels navigate with their mainsails and make headway to windward, would drive these schooners three or four quarters off course in going one to two miles—will recognize the danger which they experienced along that coast.

In 13 fathoms of water we headed for the cape, but the closer we approached the less water we found. We passed very close by it in three fathoms of water, sandy bottom, and as soon as we doubled it, there appeared a bay with a mouth three miles wide at its far end. The muddy color of the water, its lack of depth, and its

---

[8] Punta Gorda was Punta de la Bastida on other Spanish maps. It is identified as Point Grenville.

[9] San Cayetano was Ensenada de Malabrigo on other Spanish maps. It is probably what is today called Cape Shoalwater.

[10] Cape San Roque is today Cape Disappointment, the northernmost point of land forming the Entrada de Hezeta, or mouth of the Columbia River. In 1775, Hezeta had called the estuary at the mouth of the Columbia the Bahía de la Asunsión.

turbulence, would have left no doubt but that we were at the mouth of a river. Commandant Quadra had left us the map of one explored by the active American navigator Mr. Gray of the frigate *Columbia*—which name he gave to it—which agrees with the one that appeared here before us. We continued navigating with a depth of three to five fathoms, and as soon as we drew away somewhat from Cape San Roque southward, we became certain that what we beheld was the same Entrada de Hezeta because the cape appeared actually to be an island, which was one of the characteristics given for it by Don Bruno de Hezeta, its discoverer. The land in the interior of the bay, between the cape and Cape Falcon,[11] is very low, and so we consider that, because of having seen it a long distance off, it was thought to be a large mouth and that the cause of the error of latitude, which was what made us doubt, was his not having had an observation nearby to establish the latitude.

With the doubts on this point removed, the knowledge of our weakness now made a greater impression upon us. The poor characteristics of our vessels did not allow us to remain any longer along the coast than was necessary to demark its principal points. For this purpose we followed it very closely and were able, on the first good day since our departure from Nootka, to draw on the map the portion included between 46° 8' and 46° 35' latitude.

The winds continued between NW and W, though weak, and the following day gave us a clear sky and other favorable conditions for continuation of our hydrographic work. We saw Cape Foulweather[12] and to the south of it an opening, towards which we steered at full sail, intending to enter it to explore; but on drawing closer to it, we noted that the sea swelled with great force at its mouth. Nevertheless, we continued until we arrived in seven fathoms of sandy bottom and within two ship's lengths of the breakers. We saw that the channel was very narrow and impracti-

[11] So called by Bruno de Hezeta in 1775, Cape Falcon is in 45° 46' north latitude.
[12] "It was so named by the celebrated Captain Cook in remembrance of a storm that he suffered in the vicinity."—JOURNAL. [Cape Foulweather, translated by the Spaniards as Cape Mal Tiempo, was discovered by Cook on March 7, 1788.]

cable because of the surf which continued on even into the interior. On the seashore there were some huts and inhabitants.

We ran the coast southward and saw two other small mouths similar to that just mentioned. Everything examined was of medium elevation. Only to the NE of the Entrada de Hezeta could there be seen a high mountain covered with snow, which might be the origin of the Columbia River, or at least add greatly to its waters. At nightfall the wind slackened and at 10:00 P.M. we were already in a complete calm, with our only movement being from the constant swells from the west that we had felt for three days.

The morning continued the same, and we were unable to run any base lines. The sky clouded over, and at night the land breezes began and were increasing in character so that the following day it was already a fresh east wind. It kept on increasing so that we were obliged to lay to with the mainmast reefed, drawing away from the coast, which we had not seen since daybreak. After two days the sky cleared, but with the wind continuing from the SE, which, alternating with calms and southerly winds, carried us as much as 50 leagues from the coast, leaving us with only the consolation of having passed the portion seen the year before by the corvettes *Descubierta* and *Atrevida*.

As soon as the winds shifted to the third quadrant, we hauled the wind to the second quadrant, intending to return to the coast. On the nineteenth the wind blew from the fourth, and on the 20th [of September] at daybreak we were able to get within sight of land off Cape Mendocino. It is of considerable elevation and apparently formed by mountains that follow nearby along the coast as far as the eye can see.

We followed along it from the cape as far as Point Reyes when the NW wind freshened with strength and dark cloudiness. We had no other recourse but to run with it, carrying a stiff topsail in addition to the foresail so that the heavy seas would not batter the schooners. We continued that way until the afternoon of the 21st, when we sighted the Farallones of San Francisco. We were delayed in anchoring in Monterey until the 23d because the weather had turned bad on us, under which circumstances we had just those two days that were favorable for our purposes.

In Monterey they find the frigate Santa Gertrudis.[13] *The crews rest, and a map is made of the waterways that had been explored. The frigate* Aránzazu[14] *arrives, and the sloop* Ventura *is sent off to Nootka.*

There was found anchored in the port the war frigate *Santa Gertrudis,* with as its commanding officer Don Alonso Torres,[15] who had left the port of Núñez Gaona[16] on July 26 and arrived at Monterey on August 11. On the entire coast he had not been able to explore any other portion than that around the Boca de Hezeta [Columbia River], and even that was at a great distance because he had been thwarted by the weather and by a scarcity of supplies.

The port of Monterey offers a very good haven for rest and refreshment. Our crews, tired from the continual labor and the compactness of the vessels, even when in the best of health, viewed it with all the pleasure that can be expected, since they considered themselves free from the risks that could have overcome them in high latitudes and of the worry that they had upon leaving San Blas and Acapulco, at which ports a dire prediction had been made about the cruise of the schooners.[17]

[13] The *Santa Gertrudis,* a major warship, usually referred to as the *Gertrudis,* came from Spain via Peru to Mexico in late 1791 under the command of Capitán de Navío Alonso de Torres. Aboard the same ship and after a period of extended absence, Captain Juan de la Bodega y Quadra returned to the Department of San Blas.

[14] The *Aránzazu,* a frigate of 205 tons, built in the Philippine Islands port of Cavite, near Manila, came to join the San Blas fleet in 1791.

[15] See chapter 3 for more detail on the career of Captain Torres.

[16] The port of Núñez Gaona was a short-lived Spanish military settlement at Neah Bay on the south shore of the Strait of Juan de Fuca, in what is now the state of Washington. Núñez Gaona was first occupied in 1791 to solidify the Spanish presence in the Pacific Northwest. It was viewed as an alternate northern base in case Nootka, farther north, had to be turned over to the British as a result of the diplomatic negotiations that were being carried out in Europe. The location was not a very favorable one on several counts. It was abandoned by Spain in September 1792.

[17] One of the abbreviated versions of the account of the voyage of the schooners *Sutil* and *Mexicana* is found in the Archivo General de la Nación, México, D. F., in Historia, vol. 558. Seldom does this account add anything, but an exception is at this point, where the following sentence is appended: "They were given the liberty that

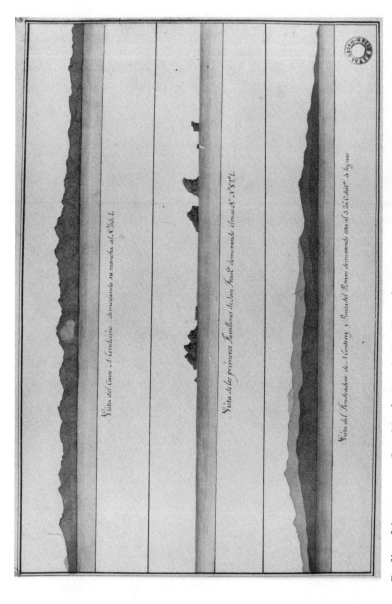

Vista del Cavo Mendocino demorando su marcha al N.½O.L.

Vista de las primeras Farallones de San Franco demorando el mar S.N.S.E.L.

Vista del Fondeadero de Monterey y Pinta del Roncro demorando esta al S. 2ª Odª. de 5 leguas.

Profiles of the coast near Cape Mendocino, the Farallones de San Francisco, and Fondeadero de Monterey, by José Cardero. Museo Naval, Madrid.

We spent the time of our stay in Monterey drawing the map of our explorations made from our departure from Nootka to our return to that port. The lack of size of our vessels had not allowed us to draw it and had limited us to piling up notes of the greatest clarity for putting them together and expanding them at the first opportunity. A room ashore provided it, and by October 24 we had already calculated and expanded the most important part of our observations concerning that area.

On October 9 the brigantine *Activa*[18] with the sloop *Ventura* entered port after nineteen days sailing from the port of Nootka, where the corvette [*sic*] *Aránzazu* had stayed under command of Lieutenant Jacinto Caamaño.[19] He had just carried out his assignment of completing the exploration of the port of Bucareli[20] and of making various others along the coast south of it, passing between it and several islands, discovering a wide channel and attaining with the means at his disposal all the advantage that could be hoped for. He was waiting for Lieutenant Salvador Fidalgo,[21] in the frigate *Princesa*,[22] to arrive at Nootka to replace him and maintain

---

their labors merited, which they repaid by behaving with propriety and good comportment."

[18] The *Activo* is listed as a brigantine of 213½ tons built in San Blas in 1792. Another vessel, known as the *Activa,* was in process of being built in 1792, being much smaller and constructed as a schooner.

[19] Lieutenant Jacinto Caamaño Moraleja was a Galician career naval officer, even though he had been born in Madrid. He became a Knight of the Order of Calatrava and served for many years in the Americas. He stayed in Mexico until 1809 and was then transferred to South America. He died, probably in Guayaquil, sometime after 1820.

[20] The Port of Bucareli in Alaska was named in honor of the viceroy of New Spain, Antonio María Bucareli y Ursúa. It is in 55° 15′ north latitude. Rather than a port, it is more appropriately the waterway between Suemez (originally Güemez) Island and Baker Island, in an area of Alaska still rich in Spanish place-names.

[21] Lieutenant Salvador Fidalgo came to San Blas in 1789 after training and service in Spain. He served both on exploratory expeditions and as temporary commandant of the Naval Department of San Blas. He was supervisor of the construction of the *Sutil*, which was built as a duplicate of the *Mexicana*, which had been built a few months earlier. During the Spanish occupation of Nootka Sound, Fidalgo served a tour of duty there as senior commander.

[22] The frigate *Princesa*, 189 tons, was constructed in the naval shipyard at San Blas in 1778.

that settlement for us until the courts of Spain and England should decide if we must give the port of Nootka to England or only the tracts of land and buildings of which they were dispossessed in 1789. Captain Vancouver,[23] with the vessels of his command, had remained at that port to await the first lunar distance [measurements] that he might obtain, because he had noted that the reckoned longitude of those he had observed up until then was very different from that reckoned by Captain Cook. During the expedition of the corvettes [*Descubierta* and *Atrevida*],[24] when we could count on longitude so exact that few other navigators will be able to equal it, both because of the different astronomical observations that we made and because of the continuous checking of the chronometers ashore, we found at once that the one reckoned by [lunar] distances [was] different from those obtained by other observations of greater confidence, by ¾ [of a degree]. Because there were many observers, and because of the repetition of many series over an interval of four days, giving a consistent error is a demonstration of having to attribute almost all of that error to the tables from which the distance is computed. Thus, far from agreeing that the longitude by [lunar] distances can be certain within ¼ of a degree, as some have contended, we could only assure it within ¾ of a degree, convinced that most often the average of several series will be within ¼ of a degree of the true longitude. This is what we told Commander Vancouver, who dismissed our proposal in favor of the ideas established in England by the best astronomers, who preferred the average of many lunar distances as an exact method of establishing longitude.

On the 22d the corvette *Aránzazu* arrived, having left at the port of Nootka the aforementioned *Princesa,* which had crossed

[23] Captain George Vancouver of the British Royal Navy also served as the commissioner sent to implement the Nootka Sound Agreement between the courts of Great Britain and Spain. He commanded the *Discovery* and the *Chatham*. His explorations carried him simultaneously into the same waters as were explored by the *Sutil* and *Mexicana* crews in the summer of 1792.

[24] In writing of the Spanish naval scientific exploratory expedition under Alejandro Malaspina, of which the *Sutil* and *Mexicana* formed a detachment, the journalist refers to the twin corvettes *Descubierta* and *Atrevida* as simply "the corvettes."

from Fuca [Núñez Gaona] with its commanding officer to occupy
the former port until receipt of new orders.

*Advice for entering the Port of Monterey. Some information is given on the
quality of the land. Of its products, both animals and plants. Of the
products of its beaches and the sea that bathes them. Of the presidio. Of the
mission. Character of the Indians. Their advancement, not only spiri-
tually but also in the cultivation of the arts and of the land. Some reflections
on the present status of this colony and on improvements that it seems could
be easily given to it. Some customs of the Runsien and Eslen Indians.*[25] *The
catechism that is taught at Mission San Carlos. Report of the status of the
missions of New California in the years {17}90 and {17}91.*

The roadstead of Monterey, located in [36° 34′ 30″] latitude and
[115° 44′ 00″] longitude offers an agreeable port of arrival for both

[25] The Runsien (or Rumsen) and Eslen (Esselen) Indians were the principal inhabitants of the Franciscan Mission San Carlos, alias Carmel. Alfred L. Kroeber, in his
Handbook of the Indians of California (Washington, D.C., 1925), pp. 463 and
545–46, identifies them as the Rumsen, a Costanoan branch of the Penutian linguistic family, and as the Esselen, who spoke a Hokan language. The noted California
anthropologist would have appreciated the information contained in the 1792 report
since he had to excuse his lack of very precise knowledge concerning both of these
groups by indicating that they were the first to become entirely extinct "and are as
good as unknown." Kroeber knew little of the Esselen and almost nothing about the
Rumsen. In the translation of the 1792 account the spellings Runsien and Eslen have
been preserved. Much of Kroeber's information on this and other California Indian
topics was expanded on the basis of more modern information and published in
Robert F. Heizer, ed., *California,* vol. 8 (Washington, D.C., 1978) of the *Handbook
of North American Indians,* a 20-volume general reference work. The Rumsen are
treated in a most general fashion by Robert Levy in his section on the Costanoan,
pp. 485–95. The entry that treats the Esselen was done by Thomas Roy Hester. In it
he states, "Clearly, the Esselen are among the least-known groups in California,"
thereby echoing what Kroeber had said more than a half century earlier. Hester
indicates that at some time in the early nineteenth century the Esselen became
culturally extinct, the first California Indians to so vanish in the post-conquest
period. The modern anthropologist pessimistically concluded that, "given the pau-
city of written data on the Esselen, archeology is the only avenue of research that may
eventually provide more information on this extinct cultural group." Hester's contribution concerning the Esselen in the *Handbook,* pp. 496–99, is much more detailed
than Levy's treatment of the Rumsen. Hester cites population estimates of 750 to
1,000 Esselen-speakers and provides a small map of the area ascribed to their aborig-
inal homeland. According to the 1792 visitors, the Esselen were much more numerous than the rival Rumsens. The Heizer *Handbook* does nothing to clarify the identity
of the Ismuracanes, the Aspaniagues, or the Vaysh groups who were mentioned by the
Spanish visitors.

the Philippine ships that sail to San Blas and Acapulco[26] and also those that, having run the Northwest Coast, are returning to the former department [of San Blas]. But the dense fog that almost always envelops it fills with anxiety the inexperienced pilot who tries to make its anchorage. To avoid the dread of this landfall, we will give notice that rarely are crosswinds experienced, that north-westerlies are as common as are the fogs, and that the strongest winds that are suffered along this coast are from the south. Therefore, whoever desires to anchor at Monterey should steer toward Point Año Nuevo and, seeing this at a distance of one mile if it is possible, steer SE ¼E [123 ¾°] until finding himself a league from Point of Pines, recognized by the many trees of this kind that cover it and by the several white spots that it has on its steep banks. Then, as one sails ESE [112 ½°], the building called the presidio will be seen to the east, and arriving in 14 fathoms, one can let go the anchor. Then it is necessary to take into account the rocks called La Loma and to use a kedge anchor astern, with which one remains in sufficient safety. But after having seen Point Año Nuevo, if one should be in the dark, either because fog blocks his view or because the light of day is disappearing, one will steer a course to approach port with little way on and, thinking himself to be at a distance from the presidio capable of being able to hear the sound of 12-calibre cannon shots, he will fire some from time to time until, hearing those that they always have ready for that purpose, the direction from which they are heard will serve as a guide for making the anchorage.

High tide is fixed at 1:30, and the water rises about eight feet.

It seems useless to speak of the configuration and anchorage of the port, since a more complete idea can be obtained by a simple examination of the map.[27]

[26] Philippine ships, in this context, were the Manila galleons that since the sixteenth century had made regular round trips from Acapulco to Manila and back, forming Spain's commercial link with the Orient.

[27] The map of Monterey Bay, done by the Malaspina main group, has been previously published in Donald C. Cutter, *Malaspina in California* (San Francisco, 1960), frontispiece. The original was engraved for the atlas volume of *Relación del viage hecho por las goletas Sutil and Mexicana en el año de 1792 . . .* (Madrid, 1802).

Tetra regio montanus, by José Cardero. Museo Naval, Madrid.

The vicinity of the port of Monterey is hilly country and broad fertile plains. The earth is made up of black, rich soil one or two feet deep over sandy, ashy clay, except close to the sea, where the shores consist at some places of shifting sands, which provide for filtration of salt that is produced here in great quantity, and in other places of granite rock with flakes of quartz, feldspar, or blackish mica, forming an angle of 80° or 90° with the horizon.

This place does not lack water as do other places in California, and here one sees groves and forests, abundant pasture, and no small number of medicinal plants and some poisonous ones. Among the different trees that are found we can name pines, oaks, poplars, and live oak.

Anonymous bird of Monterey, by José Cardero. Museo Naval, Madrid.

Gracula, by José Cardero. Museo Naval, Madrid.

Picus, by José Cardero. Museo Naval, Madrid.

The fields yield very well from the plantings of wheat, corn, legumes, and truck crops. At Mission San Carlos fruit does not fully ripen, but it does so both deliciously and abundantly at Santa Clara only 27 leagues away from it.

Although the only river that the Monterey district can count on is no less than two leagues away from the port, the frequent fogs, though inconvenient for mariners seeking it, are beneficial for its inhabitants. Without causing prejudice to health, they soften the heat of the summer sun, moisten the soil, and fertilize it to such an extent that it deceives strangers by showing in August more the pleasant appearance of springtime than the sad resemblance of summer. The naturalist of the expedition of the corvettes *Descubierta* and *Atrevida* [Tadeo Haenke] [28] was surprised to see new vege-

[28] Tadeo Haenke was a natural scientist with the Malaspina expedition and had competence in many fields. The Bohemian-born savant had visited California in

tation, both lush and general, springing forth in the month of September.

Among the wild quadrupeds to be seen are many bears of the size produced in Europe,[29] deer, stags, jackrabbits, squirrels, rats, and cottontails in such abundance that at times they can be caught by hand. The birds are ducks, turtledoves, geese, partridges, sparrows, and a quail of a graceful figure that the naturalists have named *tetrao de California*.[30]

Although the beaches are not the richest in variety of shells and snails, they certainly are as regards the beauty and value of those that they produce in abundance and that the naturalists call *Aliotis myde*.[31] The largest scarcely fit in the circle formed by touching the thumbs and forefingers of both hands together.[32] They are covered inside with a thick coating of mother-of-pearl, stained at times by a very beautiful blue cloudiness that makes them very showy.[33]

September 1791 with that group. Haenke's life and his later work in South America, where he was headquartered in Bolivia, are treated in Laurio Destefani and Donald Cutter, *Tadeo Haenke y el final de una vieja polémica* (Buenos Aires, 1966).

[29] Opposed to the opinion of Mr. Buffon . . . , 'all the animals that have been brought from Europe to America have become smaller, and those which are there on their own are also considerably smaller in America'"—JOURNAL. [Georges-Louis Leclerc (1707–88), Count of Buffon, was an aristocratic, wealthy French scientist. During his lifetime he published 36 volumes of *Histoire Naturelle*. Several additional volumes were published after his death. One of his many theses was that of degeneration of animal species in the New World environment. He obviously had not had access to specimens of the Kodiak bear, the California condor, or the Alaskan moose. Even Thomas Jefferson took an opportunity to disabuse the count by sending him a large American panther skin. A very well-written sketch of Buffon's life and contributions is found in Daniel J. Boorstin, *The Discoverers* (New York, 1983), pp. 446–57.]

[30] These quail were drawn first in 1786 by the La Pérouse expedition. Cardero, scribe and artist with the *Sutil* and *Mexicana,* did a color drawing of the California quail when he was there with Malaspina in 1791. Atanasio Echeverría added a third early depiction probably done in September or October 1792.

[31] The abalone shell was an object of great trade value. See Robert F. Heizer, "The Introduction of Monterey Shells to the Indians of the Northwest Coast," *Pacific Northwest Quarterly,* 31, 2 (1940), pp. 399–402.

[32] "A measurement determined by the Nootka Indians to be accepted as the best"—JOURNAL.

[33] "We don't know of any other beaches that compete in this precious product except those of New Zealand"—JOURNAL.

Two species of amphibians abound, sea wolves and sea otter, the skins of which, although no less dark, are of shorter hair and not as thick as is seen in those produced in high latitudes.

There also gather along this coast, and even in the anchorage, a great number of whales, but no profit can be made from them. The naturalist [José Mariano Moziño] who accompanied Don Juan de la [Bodega y] Quadra [34] and another man experienced in fishing for these animals [35] classify them in the species called *Phiseter cabodonte* and *Ballaena mistecetus;* that is, among the least oily, from the heads of which not even two ounces of sperm oil can be taken.

Various fish are caught in the port, and with ease, great quantities of sardines when they come at times to visit these shores.

These are the products that we have seen in this country. It seems to us opportune to record forthwith those noted by the members of the expedition of General Sebastián Vizcaíno [36] in December 1602 when they named this port out of respect for the Count of Monterey, [37] then viceroy of New Spain, both because on that occasion they could observe better what the spontaneous products of the soil were and also because many of the species of animals came to those places, perhaps because they were less pursued in the vicinity of the sea than in the interior of the forest.

[34] José Mariano Moziño, a Mexican scholar, wrote a fine account of his stay at Nootka with the Expedition of the Limits to the North of California. Besides publication in Spanish in 1803–4 in the *Gazeta de Guatamala* and again in Mexico in 1913, it has been translated and carefully edited by Iris Wilson [Engstrand] in *Noticias de Nutka* (Seattle, 1970).

[35] "The English captain Matthew Weatherhead, who had been engaged in the whale fishery, and who later commanding a company frigate, when leaving Tahiti, lost it on a reef that was unknown and which he located in 22°S [latitude] and 138° 30' west of London"—JOURNAL. [See chapter 3 above for more about Weatherhead.]

[36] Sebastián Vizcaíno, trader, pearl fisherman, mariner, and explorer, made the last of the early epic explorations of the California coast in 1602–3. See W. Michael Mathes, *Vizcaíno and Spanish Expansion in the Pacific Ocean, 1580–1630* (San Francisco, 1968).

[37] Gaspar de Zúñiga y Acevedo, Conde de Monterrey. Vizcaíno had a close and rewarding relationship with the viceroy count. The explorer was adroit in naming two bays in honor of his benefactor, the Bay of Monterey and the Bahía de Don Gaspar (today's Drake's Bay).

The description of this port found in the account of that expedition is as follows:

> This port is very good and well protected in all directions. It has much wood and a very great abundance of very large, straight, and clear pines for ship masts and yards. It has many and very large oaks for shipbuilding. There are rock roses, broom, roses of Castille, blackberries, willows, springs, pretty lakes, and many large and very fertile pastures and meadows for livestock, beautiful land for sown crops, with many and varied large animals. There are bears so large that their paws are a foot long and a *jeme*[38] wide. There are other animals which have hooves like mules. Some say that they are of the kind called elks. There are others as large as young bulls and built like a deer, with hair like a pelican[39] and eight inches long. They have a long neck and mane and on their head some antlers like a deer, and with a tail a vara and a half long and cloven hooves like an ox.[40] There are deer, stags, hares, rabbits, mountain lions; there are vultures, peacocks, ducks, swallows, geese and ganders; there are turtledoves, thrushes [tordos], sparrows, linnets, cardinals, quail, partridges, thrushes [zorzales], wagtails, cranes, and vultures. There are other birds like turkeys which are the largest seen on the trip. From one wing to the other they were 17 spans [12 feet].[41] There are curlews, sea gulls, crows, and many other seabirds. There are, in the sea and among the rocks, many mussels, and something like very large barnacles the shells of which are like very fine mother-of-pearl. There are oysters, lobsters, crabs, and snails. There are very large sea lions and many whales.

Both major and minor livestock brought here from the coasts of New Spain have done well in this land. They have multiplied

---

[38] A *jeme* is the distance between the thumb and the forefinger when the hand is extended to its maximum width. Clearly an imprecise measurement, it would be about six inches.

[39] Apparently the Spanish explorers were using the account of the Vizcaíno expedition published by Father Juan de Torquemada. The priest had read *pelicano* (pelican) when the original had *rabicano,* a white-tailed deer.

[40] "This seems to be what in the Monqui language the Californians call *taye*"— JOURNAL.

[41] Only the giant condor (*Gymnogyps californianus*), today a greatly endangered species with a greatly reduced habitat area, could fit this early description of 1602.

considerably, as can be seen in the report [of the status] of the missions of New California for the years [17]90 and [17]91 located at the end of this chapter.

The presidio building, which is located near the ocean in the southeast part of the port, is nothing more than a square space fenced by a low wall with a second concentric wall, in between which are the living quarters of those employed in it. The church, of the proper size and decency, is located opposite the entrance.

On the side of the presidio there is a large corral which is used to enclose livestock.

At the entrance to the building three or four bad cannons jut out to respond to [signals of] the vessels that come seeking the anchorage.

At a distance of about half a league there is a very good garden, which belongs to the governor.[42]

This is the main presidio of New California; therefore, the commander of all of them resides in it. He is normally a lieutenant colonel. The lieutenant and ensign of the 63-man company that garrisons them also live here.[43] Most are married. The presidio provides separate, though small, living quarters for each of these families. The lack of colonists of any other kind has obliged these soldiers to employ themselves in all of the occupations necessary for a civilized population. As a result, one can be seen acting as sentinel of the guard; another herding livestock, roping an animal, or driving a cart; still another building a wall, making a door, or sewing shoes; yet another arming himself to go into the interior along the roads to carry information to other presidios or missions. It would be very lengthy to express in detail all the jobs to which these soldiers, who are as good as they are neglected, lend themselves. Suffice it to say that—with a robustness perhaps due to the good climate, healthfulness of food, lack of opportunity to abandon themselves to the vice that destroys mankind, and [because]

[42] The "very good garden" of the governor was that of Pedro Fages, who from his garden had previously provided bountifully for the French naval exploring expedition under the Count of La Pérouse during its visit to Monterey in 1786.

[43] José Dario Argüello was lieutenant, and Hermenegildo Sal was ensign, of the Monterey presidial company in 1792.

Vista del Presidio de Monte Rey, by José Cardero. The version above is in the Museo Naval, Madrid; the one below is in the Robert B. Honeyman Collection, Bancroft Library, University of California, Berkeley.

Plaza del Precidio de Monte Rey. Ascribed to José Cardero; in the Robert B. Honeyman Collection.

almost all of them are of greater than average height and very strong, with admirable agility, activity, and valor—they don't have more leisure time other than that while they are standing guard. When they aren't doing this, in the hours when other things are not required of them (which are very rare), they busy themselves in domestic labors, caring for their horses, etc. Already accustomed to this continual activity, their spirits are not over-whelmed by the weight of work, but rather they enjoy with the greatest happiness the moments that they can give to diversion. With vigorous and happy spirits, they go off to the forest to hunt the cattle-destroying bears in order to kill them. They spend a great deal of the night dancing when this diversion is offered to them.

A handful of these soldiers is enough to cause troops of gentile Indians to disintegrate when they come to invade the missions, or when it is decided to punish them for having committed some treachery or other grave offense. A single one of them, without showing the least fear or reluctance, accepts the order to carry some information to another presidio, crossing hills and valleys popu-lated by enemy Indians.

But these individuals, worthy of being presented to serve as models even in the most-civilized settlements and worthy of the greatest considerations and comforts in a colony almost totally short on resources, are not even given the liberty of using their scanty salaries to choose the articles they need for their wardrobe and for their houses [by] making competitive agreements with the sellers; but rather, subject to the things that the supply officer gets for them sent under contract from New Spain, they have to accept those that he offers them and be subject to the accounts that he keeps for them.

They also live under the affliction that when the years and the continual efforts have so diminished their vigor that they are no longer capable of carrying out the tasks assigned to the troop, they are not to be permitted to make their choice to be occupied, insofar as their circumstances may permit, building a house near the presidio where perhaps their children and siblings may live, etc.,

Plaza del Precidio de Monte Rey. Ascribed to José Cardero; in the Robert B. Honeyman Collection.

Soldado de Monterey. Ascribed to José Cardero;
Museo de América, Madrid.

Mujer de un soldado de Monterey. Ascribed to José Cardero; Museo de América, Madrid.

and cultivating a piece of land which may provide them subsistence with a few comforts.

This prohibition against building houses and farming lands in the vicinity of the presidio seems contrary to that honest liberty and means of obtaining comforts to overcome the difficulties of life with which men ought mutually to help each other, the obligation being greater in proportion to the ability. Every political argument that can be proposed to defend this [present] system can easily be destroyed.

If these presidial soldiers were permitted, even while still serving, to be able to gradually use their financial savings and the time that is not specifically required in their military duties to build up an estate and raise some livestock to give comfort to their families and for the time when they are required to retire because of an unfortunate occurrence, the weight of years, or the desire for repose, having completed the term of their enlistment, they would find a means to subsist without being subject to beggary and seeing them submerged in misery after having led a wearisome life exposed to the greatest dangers. Then in a very few years one would see a flourishing colony created on this fertile landscape, useful for its inhabitants and of comfort and recreation for the mariners, in particular those of the Philippine vessel that should touch at this port. These individuals, who with happy faces rush quickly into the continual duties that are given to them, no matter how dangerous and bothersome, not permitting them any more hours of rest than those necessary, showing the greatest concern for the conservation of the king's property and at times of his officers, with how much care and industriousness would they work on their small properties, fruit of their efforts, for the comfort of their families?

The regard that these useful vassals of the king show us has motivated us to enlarge perhaps too much on this subject; but knowing that it is not up to us to form the political system that it seems should be established in this colony, we will stop talking about this subject and go on to deal with the mission.

Near the banks of the Carmel [River] and the seashore, and about two leagues from the presidio, is the mission of San Carlos

[Borromeo]. Its buildings are a moderate-sized church, the hospice for the religious with accompanying offices, one storeroom for the shipments and farm tools and another for the grain, a small house for the corporal and four or five soldiers assigned to the mission guard [44] and for other necessary uses. It was founded in 1770. It is administered by three apostolic missionaries of Propaganda Fide of the College of San Fernando de México. [45] One of these is the president of all the missions of New California, named Fray Fermín de Lasuén. These religious deserve the praise and acquired the affection of all members of the expedition of the corvettes *Descubierta* and *Atrevida* because of their modesty, piety, austerity of customs, diligence in providing for the spiritual good of the natives, and their graciousness of conduct. They deserved from us of the schooners no lesser indication of the greatest esteem, and we found very clear evidence of the appreciation shown to this small congregation of virtuous men by those of the unfortunate expedition of Mr. La Pérouse.

With flattery and presents they attract the savage Indians and persuade them to adhere to life in society and to receive instruction for a knowledge of the Catholic faith, the cultivation of land, and the arts necessary for making the instruments most needed for farming.

In proof of this it will not be out of place to cite an example that gives evidence of the zeal and tenderness of the father president [Lasuén] and of the inclination of the savages.

The leader of one of these pagan tribes, as respected for his valor as he was loved by his people for the natural talents he possessed, was at death's door. He had shown esteem for the father president, and I don't know whether or not he had done him some kindness.

---

[44] "The assignment of the four soldiers and a corporal which each mission has from the nearby presidio resulted from the invasion made in 1775 by the Indians at Mission San Diego, burning it and killing a missionary [Fr. Luis Jaume]"—JOURNAL.

[45] The three Franciscan priests were Father President Fermín Francisco de Lasuén of Vitoria, Alava, a Basque; Pascual Arenaza, likewise a Basque from Alava province; and José Señán, a Catalan from Barcelona, who many years later became prelate of the California missions. The Malaspina group always referred to Lasuén as Matías rather than Fermín.

Misión del Carmelo de Monterey. Ascribed to José Cardero; in the Robert B. Honeyman Collection.

When the latter learned of the sad situation of the former on a stormy night of constant rain, despite his dwelling place being some leagues away, he went there for the purpose of persuading him not to depart this world without embracing the Catholic faith and purifying himself with holy baptism. After great difficulty he arrived at last to talk with him, and having made known to him the reason for his trip and of the ardent desire that he had that a person whom he loved would not be lost forever, but rather, by trying to persuade him of the truth of what he was telling him and subjecting him to the ceremonies required by Christianity, he would obtain the reward that is promised to those who duly profess it. Then the pagan, being convinced, said to the father president: "I believe what you tell me and I will do what you direct because I find that no other interest but what you tell me can have motivated you to leave the comforts of your home to travel a number of leagues on a stormy night; I am convinced of your good will and I place myself in your hands." [46]

[46] The story was heard earlier including a sequel. As an illustration of the capacity for gratitude demonstrated by the local Indians, the writer of the Malaspina account gave two examples. The second concerned the old chief whom Lasuén had visited on a stormy night. The Indian rancheria was over 20 miles distant from Carmel Mission. Nevertheless, after the aged Indian's recovery from the grave illness that had prompted Lasuén's trip, the unnamed chief, despite his advanced age, went personally to the mission to let it be known how much the memory of past visits had inspired him and to express the hope that these would not be lacking in the future. The other

One of the religious is in charge of instructing the converts and the children in the Spanish language and in the dogma of our religion, and the other of the direction and instruction in cultivation of the soil, the mechanical skills, and domestic service, taking care that those who are well taught teach the others, and obliging all to observe the rules established by the father president. Much to our satisfaction, we noticed several young Indians who served in the temple with decorum and respect, comparing their happy lot with the status of their companions wandering through the forests, without enlightenment, without religion, given over to the impulse of their passions and the misery of savage life.[47] We also saw with pleasure the great attention with which the Indians care for the religious. They prepare their meals and serve at the table

---

story was of a pagan boy who one afternoon received some beads from Lasuén. The boy returned the following day with his father to give the priest a large quantity of *pinole* in repayment. Corbetas, tomo 6, MS 95 in Museo Naval, f. 246. Novo y Colson, ed., *Viaje político-científico alrededor del mundo . . .* , p. 446, says *piñones* (pine nuts) rather than *pinole* (ground parched corn), apparently in a misreading of the original manuscript.

[47] "'Man in a rude and savage state with a precarious subsistence exposed to the inclemencies of the seasons, and the fury of wild beasts is an object of pity, when compared to a man enlightened and assisted by philosophy'—William Nicholson, *Natural Philosophy.*"—JOURNAL. [William Nicholson, English chemist and physicist (1753–1815), was founder of the *Journal of Natural History*. He also wrote frequently for *Philosophical Transactions*.]

without it being necessary to prompt them frequently what they should do. At the hours of prayer and instruction, the children's choir resounded as it intoned the prayers of the church; they recited the part of the catechism that they knew and repeated the words of that part they still didn't know, which the catechist kept on telling them with the greatest of patience.

The Indians who come to this mission, whether they are of the Runsien, Eslen, Ismuracanes, or Aspaniagues tribes,[48] are all of medium stature, dark color, and seem to be the stupidest as well as the ugliest and dirtiest that can be found, corresponding in great measure to the description that the editor of Father Venegas's history gives concerning the character of the natives of [Baja] California in the following words:

> The basis of the character of the Californians is composed of stupidity and insensibility; lack of knowledge and reflection; inconsistency and fickleness; of a will and of appetites without control, without knowledge and even without objective; laziness and terror of all work; perpetual adhesion to all types of pleasure and to childish and brutal entertainment; fearfulness and weakness of spirit; and finally, a miserable lack of everything that makes men, that is, rational, political, and useful to themselves and to society.[49]

Having cited this description, which seems to us sufficiently accurate but very unfavorable to those natives, it is proper to remember what Captain Vizcaíno says about them as the result of the first visit of Spaniards to the savages of Monterey: "The entire port is sur-

[48] The Malaspina group in its investigations a year earlier had concluded that there were three tribes united at San Carlos, "The Runsien, the Eslen, and the Vaysh." Their neighbors on the north, towards Missions Santa Clara and San Francisco, were the "Ymuaracen" and the "Aspasniac." Novo y Colson, ed., *Viaje,* p. 443.

[49] Jesuit Father Miguel Venegas had written his *Noticia de la California* based on records of Jesuit activity in Baja California. It was published anonymously in three volumes in Madrid, Spain, in 1757 in an edition prepared by another Jesuit, Father Andrés Burriel. Two years later, in 1759, an English-language version was published in London in two volumes, but the translation was defective. There have been subsequent translations into other languages. This Jesuit work is mentioned frequently in the 1792 account. The explorers lean heavily on it, frequently to the point of merely seconding what had been said decades earlier about an area and about Indians over a thousand miles distant. *Noticia de la California* 1:74.

rounded by rancherias of agreeable Indians, and very willing, and who like to give what they have: They use bows and arrows and have their own system of government." Though we confess that the stupidity of these natives is very common, we should not for that reason consider them incapable of work that requires reflection and judgment. The stupidity that we blame on them seems to be more an obstruction of their powers by lack of usage, combined with an innate laziness that bothers even their thinking, rather than a limit of the same, so that when they are put in motion and when they are gradually given ideas, they don't fail to discuss them and, although not with the greatest quickness or perfection, they learn what is taught them. They cultivate the field, they care for livestock, they make bricks, they build buildings, they make tools, works of carpentry, and so on.

The method they have of hunting deer is exceedingly industrious. They keep the skins of some heads of these animals with their horns and part of the neck, and skinned with much care. Next they fill these with dry grass, trying to conserve the shape they had when they were attached to the head. On going out to hunt, they fit these caps over their heads, and situated in a convenient place, they stand on three "feet," including the left hand. With the right hand they have their bow and arrow ready, and as soon as they see one of those animals, they note whether it is male or female and, as soon as they know, they try to imitate the movements appropriate to the opposite sex, which they do with such perfect similarity that, by attracting it within range, they fire the arrow that rarely fails to have the sought-after effect.

Nor does laziness reach the point that they are not stimulated to hasten work that has been given them in the hope of some presents or the desire to eat well for several days or to get some clothing to cover themselves. When in the presidio they need considerable quantities of roof tiles or bricks for the buildings, they announce to the nearby savage tribes that, if some Indians want to go and occupy themselves in these tasks, they will be given a blanket and they will be given daily the meat and boiled corn that they need. Many accept this proposal and offer to take part. They choose those who seem best, and they come on the appointed day; they present themselves to the governor, they turn over to him their bows and arrows, they receive their blankets, and they start to work.

Situated on a little elevation northeast of the hospice or mission house are the dwellings of the Indians. Each of these is little more than a small enclosure of stones or adobes covered with branches or straw, little better than those that the editor [of Venegas's history] describes, and having the same aversion that he tells us about living in houses with roofs:

> In the rest of the land their houses are nothing more than a small enclosure of stone piled up a half vara high and a vara square, with no other roof than the sky, houses truly so narrow and humble that in comparison to them one could call a tomb a palace. Within this house they cannot lie down and it is necessary for them to sleep seated inside that small enclosure. It is true that at the principal missions they have made some houses to please the priests, but many don't live in them, nor is there any way to persuade them to do so, because they become anguished under a roof.[50]

We wanted to know from the father president [Lasuén] why these Indians were not directed and given the means to improve their houses in order to protect themselves from the inclemency of the weather. He told us that they just continued not wanting to live in them, preferring to live in the open.

The men, with the exception of those employed in the principal occupations such as majordomo, sacristan, blacksmith, carpenter, and so on, go around undressed in summer, with nothing more than modesty indispensably requires. The Indian women have tied to their waists a fringe made of palm leaves or dry grass that reaches their knees, and over the shoulders a cape of coarse cloth or of sea otter skins with which they cover their bodies to the knees.

The religious ardently desire to have the means of dressing better these unfortunates, but up to now it hasn't been granted them as in some other missions of New California, where minor livestock have increased so that with wool they have material

[50] Venegas, *Noticia de la California* 1 : 89.

India y Indio de Monterey, by José Cardero. Museo Naval, Madrid.

Indio de Monterey. Ascribed to José Cardero; Museo de América, Madrid.

enough to weave blankets and to dress almost all the Indians, as happens at San Buenaventura.

The stipends of the religious, which are 400 *pesos fuertes* a year for each one, are collected by the syndic of the missions in Mexico [City]. With them they fill the requisitions of the missionaries. These are transported 160 leagues overland to the department of San Blas and 500 by sea to Monterey.[51] Although the costs of freight and damages are paid by the king, and the missionaries are reduced voluntarily to very few necessities, having more than they need with half that amount, there is not enough with what is left over for the principal needs that the Indians have. Furthermore, not all of it is used at the choice of those missionaries, but only the portion that is not used in the spiritual and temporal conquests. Thus beforehand they order blankets, medicine, and tools because they know what is most useful for them, and later they receive whatever they want to send them.

[51] The role of the Spanish naval base is well developed in Michael E. Thurman, *The Naval Department of San Blas: New Spain's Bastion for Alta California and Nootka Sound, 1767–1798* (Glendale, Calif., 1967).

Since presents are the most essential thing that the missionaries need to use as eloquence to attract and persuade the Indians, it is necessary for them to have the materials to be able to make them. By this means they induce them to live in society under instruction to receive religion, and at times to cease making war with those against whom they have some complaint.

The religious have lacked some resources which had been given to them in the zeal of the first settlements. Even though the sovereign has always been kind and liberal for the continuation of a work so worthy of the support of a monarch as is the conversion of a great number of our fellow men who inhabit the coast, miserable for lack of learning, worried by a thousand superstitions, given over to a roving life and to all of the discomforts that accompany it, foraging at times like animals, accustomed to destroy each other by continual wars for frivolous reasons, to the pleasure of social life, to a knowledge of the true religion, and to the means of alleviating the discomforts that inclemency of weather causes us and of receiving the necessary food for our sustenance with some gratefulness, those delegated by His Majesty for providing, with prudent attention, for the most necessary help for these zealous missionaries perhaps have not carried it out with that care that such a great work requires. This reprehensible neglect has caused them many needs. The following example can serve as proof: Mr. La Pérouse, commander of the French expedition, sympathizing with the need in which these religious found themselves in having to grind wheat with metates to knead the bread that they were to eat, gave the mission a very well-made wooden mill. It only lacked a small stone to reap the benefit of that present so worthy of remembrance. But the repeated and humble pleas of the president have not been enough to obtain this benefit from the administrators.

Though it seems these needs could discourage the religious involved in the spiritual conquest, these obstacles are impotent to them with their ardent charity, and seeing the progress that the thirteen existing missions have had, they request the founding of an additional one between any two of them to gather in the intermediate pagans.

We know very well that a true philosopher, in considering the system of temporal government that is followed at these missions, would find many defects and wouldn't hesitate to propose a much more appropriate plan for attracting the Indians not only to a social life, to ground them in the Christian religion, to instruct them in the rights of man and in mutual obligations, but also in the way of acquiring some comforts. However, we are very much persuaded that with difficulty would they find for the execution of the plan the needed number of subjects of a good heart, true Christians, talented, with winning manners or the gentility to ingratiate themselves and make themselves loved, as free of vile interests as they are untiring in obtaining true happiness for others, with the necessary knowledge for this, and who might want to be employed in an enterprise that is so rough and full of difficulties.

In view of these circumstances we believe that the conversion or instruction of the natives of New California ought not to be entrusted to any other hands than those of the religious in which it is found. Motivated certainy by religious zeal, they enter the exemplary College of San Fernando de México. In this virtuous school they are purified and go off to the conquest adorned in the beautiful robe of charity.

Nevertheless, we must confess that in that College of San Fernando they should equip the catechists with the proper instruction for making the Californians not only Christians but also useful to society and the state, to provide them with an enjoyable life and to lead them to religion along broad and flowery paths. The subjects sent to California should be taught methodically under good teachers the languages of those barbarian nations with whom they are to deal. They should have instilled in them, in their inclinations and customs, the methods that have produced the best results for the purposes of conversion and civilization. And since they are to be the directors of physical efforts, they should have acquired a knowledge of agriculture, stock raising, the tools most useful for the cultivation of the fields, the easiest way to spin, weave, and so on. There they should deal with what are the best ways to overcome the laziness of the Indians, a result of custom and a product of circumstances, this horror that they imagine concerning work, this idleness as origin of their vices and one of the causes of their wars. Those who deal with this subject should bear in mind that as long as man does not become convinced that the advantage he enjoys from a thing is greater than the difficulty that he has been caused in getting it, he will never undertake the means to come into possession of it. Considering also that there are many things that in order to acquire a fondness for them it is not enough to use them only once. It must be that, at times forcibly at first, that what on the first trials they disliked, later it becomes a necessity for well-being. The trick is in making man like certain things for which, experience has showed us, if used for a certain time, he gains a liking that makes them a necessity. By supplying them without effort on their part, or at least with very little, and when they realize that they are already accustomed and that they can no longer do without them, then to teach them the way to acquire them and leave them alone. The viceroy on one hand and the ecclesiastical prelate on the other should agree to establish and promote this plan of education, if, as one should assume, they have the necessary ideas for it.

Up to now it has been customary in the missions to oblige all the Indians to work for everyone, without permitting property to anyone, both because this system has seemed more suitable to the brotherhood and union that should reign in a small society and because they had experienced that those to whom a plot of ground had been assigned cared very little for its cultivation, if not abandoning it altogether. This system would merit some reflection and ought to be tried with greater attention to see if the assignment of property with convenient help would cause some stimulus to work and to industry.

We will conclude this chapter by giving to the public a report of some of the customs or religious ideas of the two nations—the Eslen and the Runsien—which it has been possible to investigate by means of various questions to the neophytes who already have some knowledge of our language.

It seems that the number of Eslenes was greater than that of the Runsienes. They both lived scattered under the direction of some chiefs, to whom, if they gave some subordination, it was in the continual wars that they had with the neighboring nations. Therefore this distinction or authority was not achieved except through valor and talent. The men went about undressed,[52] and the women covered in the most essential parts, foraging amid the fields like beasts or gathering seeds for winter while they were still green, and when those were exhausted, they busied themselves in hunting and fishing, particularly for shellfish.

Those who are in the mission have not yet lost fondness for such [native] foods, for we have seen a girl chew with considerable pleasure stalks of the most tasteless plants; and despite being aided by those provided by the mission, they gather a great quantity of the seeds to which they are accustomed. The one they like best is the one they call *teda*. To eat those that they use in place of bread, they toast them in trays by throwing heated stones over the seeds and mixing these with them until they get them to the proper point. Then they grind them in wooden mortars, very well made by them; and now that they have instruments with which to do it easily and know the advantage, they boil them and leave them to form pap. We tried it and found it to be rather palatable to the taste.

When specific needs do not require them to be occupied, they take the greatest delight in lying face down and spending several hours that way, a pleasure which is noted in them even at the mission.

Convinced certainly by human perversion, they value power more than any other accomplishment. They know that superiority

[52] "The Californians are so used to living naked that the editor of the history by Father Venegas says that for them to see one of their fellow countrymen dressed was a spectacle of such laughter as it would be among us to see a monkey dressed. Modesty was so unknown among the men that they took it as an affront and a dishonor at first when they were forced to go about dressed. In this matter they had so little apprehension that, as Father Juan María Salvatierra says, they were scandalized when at first the priests ordered them to cover themselves, at least as much as prudence requires, not being able to find in themselves the indecency that they were taught about their nudity."—JOURNAL. [This is a partial quotation from Venegas, *Noticia de la California* 1:87. Father Salvatierra was an Italian Jesuit priest and founder of early missions in Baja California.]

in power should free them from attack by their neighbors and give warning against insults.

Their wars are of as little boldness and duration as are their truces, which are of little confidence, since only the memory that there have been killings and robberies puts arms into their hands; and at times the whim of the chiefs is enough to start hostilities.

It doesn't seem extraneous to record what the editor of Father Venegas's work says in describing the character of the Californians farther south for the analogy we find between them and those with whom we are dealing. His words are as follow:

The movement of their will is commensurate with their lack of intelligence, and all their passions have very short sphere. They have no ambition and what they like best is to be considered not so much as valiant as for being considered strong. The desire of fame is not attractive to them, nor do they long for preeminence in order to command. They do not know about either, so neither exists, or this powerful spring that is the motive in this world for so many works both bad and good is misplaced or unused among them. The most that is found in them is some sense of rivalry or emulation. They are vexed at seeing their companions praised or rewarded, and only this puts them into some action and makes them shake off the laziness that they innately have. Nor does the corrosion of avarice dwell in their hearts. Their desires extend only as far as obtaining food for today without much work, and they don't work anxiously to assure it for tomorrow. Their concern for possessions is no greater than for those miserable trinkets that they use for adornment, for fishing, for hunting, or for war. Finally, their covetousness for property and possessions is like that of those who have no house nor home, nor any kind of land of the fields, nor divisions nor fractions of these; nor do they know any rights than that of being the first one to pick the fruits that the land spontaneously produces.

This state of mind both gives them a prodigious laziness and languidity, in which they spend their life in idleness and inaction and with a horror of any work or effort, and also makes it easy to let themselves be attracted to the first thing their fancy or outside influence proposes to them and also to change their minds with equal ease. They conceive aversion and hate and become inflamed to vengeance over the slightest causes, but for the same causes, or even without them, they become appeased after having taken vengeance, and even sometimes before so doing. It is enough for them to strike whoever resists them, because although nothing appears to be of any value to them except valor, it can be said that in them there is not a trace of true valor. Their animosity lasts only as long as it takes to find a greater one. The least thing is enough to frighten them, and there is nothing unbecoming to them as soon as they begin to yield and fear takes hold of their spirits. But on the contrary, their pride has no limit if they gain some advantage or if the enemy is intimidated or shows some weakness.

They always attack by surprise or treachery, but the deaths for each attack are few, since when two or three fall the others retreat and return to their false friendship, to their coalition houses, their invitations, dances, and games.

Sometimes grudges between different tribes were decided by challenge. After the day and place were settled, the chiefs advised their subordinates, and they came with a bow, arrow, and leather jacket, smeared with ochre and adorned with feathers. They were usually followed by their wives and children, but with the precaution of remaining hidden at some distance from the place of battle to make flight easier or to share in the celebration of victory, according to whether the results of the dispute were unfavorable or favorable. It was generally accompanied by a martial chant, alternating with shouts. The combatants formed two lines, and the distance for starting the skirmish with arrows was only about ten paces.

Since one of their principal strategems for winning was always to intimidate the enemy, each side tried to do so by making the other side hear the battle preparations and by making the consequences of the first victory horrible by stripping off with great eagerness and speed the skins of the first victims and displaying them stretched out between two poles.[53]

We have been able to acquire very little knowledge about the religious ideas of the Runsienes and the Eslenes, either because they were very limited and there were very few of them, or because

[53] Venegas, *Noticia de la California* 1 : 75–78.

the missionaries showed abhorrence in hearing the story of their beliefs and they had been intimidated and set aside the telling about it.

We have only been able to learn that the former [the Runsienes] believed that the sun was of a similar nature to themselves; that is, that he was a man and that he had the power to take their lives. The latter [the Eslenes] believed that after this life everyone was transformed into *tecolotes,* or owls, a bird to which they showed a singular veneration. [54]

No idolatry has been found among the Californians. Neither temples, nor altars, nor places set aside for religious rites have been seen unless one considers as such the one that those of the voyage of Sebastián Vizcaíno supposed was a temple on Santa Catalina Island.

These two nations of which we are speaking are no less devoted to their dances than those of the south. The already-cited editor, speaking of these, says:

It is not strange that they should be advanced in this occupation of dancing since it is the only one that they have in peacetime. It is natural to be advanced in what one always does. They amuse themselves and dance for weddings, for good luck in fishing and hunting, for the birth of their children, for celebrating their harvests, for victories over their enemies, or for any other causes the gravity of which they would not pause greatly in weighing or examining. For these celebrations they usually invite several rancherias and also compete often in wrestling, jumping, and run-

[54] "The Edues that inhabit part of Old California also give a conspicuous place to owls, since a missionary referring to the false belief of the Southern Edues, or Pericués, cites the report made by them that begins thus: 'That in the heavens lives a lord whom they call Niparaya, who made the earth and the sea. He gives food; he created the trees and everything that we see and he can do whatever he wants. This said Niparaya has a wife called Anaricondis, and although he doesn't have sex with her, because he has no body, they have had three children. One of these is Quayayp, who is a man, and Anayicondi gave birth to him in the Sierras of Acaragui. Said Quayayp lived among those Indians of the south and taught them. He was powerful and had many people because he entered into the earth and brought out people. They got mad at him and killed him and when they killed him they put on him a veil of thorns. Today he is dead, but very beautiful, without any corruption, continually bleeding. He doesn't talk because he is dead, but he has a *tecolote* (or owl) who speaks to him . . ., etc.'"—JOURNAL. [Venegas, *Noticia de la California* 1 : 102].

ning, in tests of strength, and skill with the bow and arrow. In
these and other entertaining games they frequently spend days,
weeks, and months in time of peace.[55]

Since the missionaries try to make the discipline that they use
with the converts, or with those ready for conversion, the easiest
possible, they don't prohibit some of them from going to those
festivals to which some of their pagan relatives come to invite them.

Among the Runsienes and Eslenes each man was permitted no
more than one wife,[56] and their infidelities were neither punished
nor hardly even heeded; with the former being careful, nevertheless, to punish severely the accomplice of an adulterer with sticks,
wounds, and incisions, from which once in a while she died.
Whereas among the second group [Eslenes] it was not only common to repudiate the woman and then even later to readmit her in
her same status, but also she was given at times by the first
husband to the new lover, if both transgressors desired it and the
latter gave the beads and other goods that the former had given to
the family for her purchase.

This method of buying wives[57] was common to both nations,
although among the Runsienes the intervention of the families of

[55] Venegas, *Noticia de la California* 1 : 96.

[56] "Among the Edues, or Pericués, of the South there was polygamy. The women
looked after the family sustenance and, in competition, brought fruit and seeds of the
woods to their husbands to make them content, because once outcast (a thing that
depended solely on his fancy), they couldn't easily find anyone who would admit
them. There was no such excess among the nation at Loreto, where only a few of the
principal men had two wives, the rest of them living with only one. Adultery was
looked upon as a sin that at least gave just motive for revenge, except for two
occasions. One was their fiestas and dances, and the other was their fights, in which
sometimes one or another rancheria challenged each other so that on these [occasions]
such was the shameful prize of the victor"—JOURNAL. [Venegas, *Noticia de la California* 1 : 92—93.]

[57] "The method of marriage bargaining of the Loreto Nation was for the suitor to
present to his intended a tray, which in their Monqui Indian language they call Olo,
woven of mescal thread. If accepted, it was a sign of consent, and she had to return to
the suitor a mesh bag; and with this mutual giving of things of value the marriage
became celebrated"—JOURNAL. [Venegas, *Noticia de la California* 1 : 93.]

the sweethearts made the contract much more solemn, those of the man contributing with their share for the purpose, which was divided between those of the bride at the time of handing her over.

They show signs of tenderness toward their children, and like sensitive people, they never leave them, not even in their most tiring occupations, but rather they are frequently seen loaded down with their little ones. They are loving mothers, and they are not indifferent nor unfaithful wives. Very few weaknesses are noted, and they seem to be attentive in fulfilling their duties. The women in general are fertile and strong. In California it is not rare to give birth in the field and for the new mother to undertake her tasks as soon as she has successfully given birth.[58]

Robbery was a crime almost unknown to both nations. Among the Runsienes they also look at the killing of another person with indifference. It is not so with the Eslenes, who punish the delinquent the same way [with death] unless he acted with the permission of the chief, which he had asked for and which is usually given when there is a disturber of public tranquility.

The funeral services that accompany the death of a chief are not equal but similar. Only the family or the entire tribe get together to cry around the corpse, cutting their hair and throwing ashes over their faces. At this ceremony, which at times lasts four days, they keep giving out clothing and beads, dividing finally among the family the few things that comprised the property of the deceased. The Eslenes, on the contrary, did not distribute anything, but rather all of [the chief's] friends and subjects had to contribute some beads, which were burned with him.

We shouldn't stop speaking of the customs of the Indians who are present at Mission San Carlos without reporting on one that the

[58] "Among the Californians of the South is found the custom that the recent mothers go off immediately to the water to bathe and to wash their babies, acting in every other way without any caution, going to the forest for wood, looking for food, and working in everything else that the husband should be doing. Meanwhile he plays the role of the tired and suffering one, retiring to his cave or lying under a tree very protected for three or four days."—JOURNAL. [This custom, with various modifications, was widely diffused along the Pacific Coast. It is referred to as the couvade. See Kroeber, *Handbook of the Indians of California,* passim.]

father president [Lasuén] said had been noted among them from the time of arrival of the religious in that place, and which they continue, the religious not having opposed it because it was not considered contrary to morality.

These natives make a circular trench in the ground and then they cover it with a bell-shaped hood, leaving a very narrow door as an entrance to that room, making it an oven. On one side of it they throw some firewood which they burn at the proper time. When the men come in from work, they go off to that heater, which is already prepared with the proper fire. They enter gradually up to the number that it can hold, while those who have to wait amuse themselves with various games.

Those who are inside suffer that unnatural heat that there is inside the heat chamber until they sweat a great deal; when they leave, they scrape their skin with the edge of a shell for that purpose, taking off with the sweat the filth that covers them. Afterwards they bathe in the river and on coming out they wallow in the dirt.[59]

We have not been able to learn whether this action is taken by them as a health preservative or as a means of giving rest to the body.

Since it seems to us that to inquisitive people there would be no lack of interest in knowing how far the missions have been able to progress in the instruction of the Indians in the principles of our religion, we will next record the part of the Christian doctrine that the reverend father missionaries teach the catechumens and neophytes at Mission San Carlos.

When the *capitán de navío* and commanding officer [Torres] of the frigate *Santa Gertrudis* wrote a letter to the father president of that mission [Lasuén], thanking him for assistance that he owed to

[59] The sweathouse, known as the *temescal,* was a very common institution among the various Indian groups of California.

[60] "It is very noteworthy that in neighboring nations, and without specific boundaries, there is such a great difference in languages, from which one can infer the difference in the origins of settlement of these lands"—JOURNAL. [The thirty-one items marked with an x appear in the printed version of the *Relación* published in 1802. In square brackets are any divergent spellings.]

Dictionary of the Runsien and Eslen Languages[60]

Spanish	Runsien	Eslen	[English]
x uno	enjalá	pek	[one]
x dos	ultis	u-lhaj	[two]
x tres	kappes	julep	[three]
x quatro	ultitum (English t) [ultizim]	jamajus	[four]
x cinco	hali-izu	pe-majalá	[five]
x seis	hali-shakem	pegualanai	[six]
x siete	kapkamai-shakem	jula-jualanai	[seven]
x ocho	ultumai-shakem	julep-jualanai	[eight]
x nueve	pakke	jamajus-jualanai	[nine]
x diez	tam-chajt	tomoila	[ten]
once	—	petelenais	[eleven]
doce	—	jula-elenay	[twelve]
trece	—	julep-elenay	[thirteen]
catorce	—	jamaj-elenay	[fourteen]
quince	—	masnak-elenay	[fifteen]
diez y seis	—	peshish	[sixteen]
veinte	—	pek efejedes	[twenty]
treinta	—	julep-tomoila	[thirty]
x hombre	muguyamk	ejenutek [Ejennutek]	[man]
x muger	latziyamank [latriyamank]	tanutek	[woman]
x hijo	enshinsh	panna	[son]
x hija	kaana	tapanna	[daughter]
muger mia	kajaguan	nitsekta	[my wife]
marido mio	kaurrin	nitseheké	[my husband]
x mio	ká [ka]	nitschá	[mine, my]
x tuyo	me	nimetahá	[your, yours]
x dia sol [dia]	ishmen	asatzá	[day, sun]
rayo del sol, resplandor	sushpú	ashi	[sunbeam]
x luna	orpetuei-ishmen	tomanis-ashi	[moon]
x noche	orpetuei	tomanis	[night]
estrellas	pajarras	atimulai	[stars]
x grande	ishac	putuki	[large]
x chico	pishit	ojusk	[small]
x padre	appan	a-hay	[father]
x madre	aán	a-zia [Azia]	[mother]
suegro	paap	lashaú	[father-in-law]
x hermano	taan	mi-itz	[brother]
hermana	tá	—	[sister]
hermano menor	tauchens	—	[younger brother]
x fuego	hëllo [hello]	ma-mamanes	[fire]
x luz	shortó [shorto]	jétza [jetza]	[light]
x agua	ziy	azanax	[water]
ballena	tim (English t)	pushuc, pashishis	[whale]
nutria	shustu	c'chitfu	[sea otter]
lobo marino	tominsh	op-obus	[sea lion]

Spanish	Runsien	Eslen	[English]
oso	arresh	coltála	[bear]
liebre	cheish	samás	[hare]
conejo	werren	chish	[rabbit]
hardilla [*sic*]	hef	mexé	[squirrel]
leon	heksh	jekess	[lion]
perro	matchá	shootsh	[dog]
gato montes	hôm	tolloma	[mountain lion]
x cielo	terraj	imita	[sky]
x arco	laguan	payunaj	[bow]
x flecha	teps	lottós	[arrow]
pedernal	tip	cumaltéss	[flint]
morir	lakun	chuneipa	[to die]
matar	nim	hik-ké	[to kill]
robar	attay	ju-ma	[to rob]
robado	meatiyan	—	[robbed, stolen]
fornicar	yappé	tesmasha	[to fornicate]
preñada	paish	sallamasek	[pregnant]
parir	yziu	aozapá	[to give birth]
año	shiiu	—	[year]
piel	chitlul	ze-kesh	[skin]
x amigo	kauk	mish-fé [mish-fe]	[friend]
comer	amjai	ampa	[to eat]
beber	hukesh	etze	[to drink]
yerba	hun	amitchana	[grass]
flor	tiush	hy-i	[flower]
raiz	hektó	ypi-mi	[root]
monte	hutcha	pol-lomo	[forest, mountains]
llano	turk	ayola	[plain]
nieve	yokop	matzeijó	[snow]
salmon	urrak	killiuay	[salmon]
sardina	tupun	tupur	[sardine]
pescar	urk	takaldama	[to fish]
cazar	punni	takampa	[to hunt]
escrivir	enn	chempa (pintar)	[to write]
cipres	zummir	zummir	[cypress]
pino (no tienen nombres genericos de arboles, pescados, etc.)	yx	yx-aý	[pine tree (they don't have generic names for trees, fish, etc.)]
enfermo	yin	matochis	[sick]
madera	moyór	y-i	[lumber]
cavello	hutt	hakká	[hair]
casa	rukka	aúa	[house]
caveza	chojon	hatasex	[head]
ojos	xin	sixpa	[eyes]
narices	huis	hoské	[nose]
boca	hayé	yshi	[mouth]
lengua	lasf	villel	[tongue]

Dictionary of the Runsien and Eslen Languages (*continued*)

Spanish	Runsien	Eslen	[English]
dientes	zit	ahui	[teeth]
orejas	tuxús	tuxús	[ears]
cuello	katká	wowel	[neck]
pecho	tuká	shejosáf	[chest]
brazos	yzú	jushú	[arms]
manos	talt	tallanu	[hands]
dedos	tursi	tu-chullis	[fingers, toes]
corazon	rutzushim	tikass	[heart]
barriga	pittin	ytyanef	[belly]
pellejo	turrúm	zek-jass	[skin]
tripas	redas	abjazcú	[intestines]
miembro viril	pilliu	ka we	[penis]
testiculos	shokask	—	[testicles]
muslos	payan	wek hée	[thighs]
piernas	corró	pi-yáss	[legs]
pies	tult	nenepassuf	[feet]
uñas	uatcharim	olloja	[nails]
hueso	chatchie	hiyá	[bone]
sombrero	chepels	pamukó	[hat]
canasto, donde cuesen	zuié	apitmakiy	[basket, in which they cook]
canoa	canon	—	[canoe]
piedra	yrrex	yllex	[stone]

his care and hospitality and telling him of the admiration and edification that he felt in finding the Indians under his care so well instructed both in the Spanish language and in the knowledge of our beliefs, he responded to that commander, placing at the end of the letter a note in the following terms:

> The Mission of Carmel is a mixture of Indians of the Eslen and Runsien languages, which two nations are so opposite from each other that it costs infinite effort to reconcile the two because their ill will is reciprocal. It is no less difficult for the missionaries to instruct them in the two languages in order to teach the Indians in them.[61]

There follows the catechism in the best way that it has been possible to arrange it, and what is most essential for their salvation,

[61] The Rumsen and Esselen Indians were indeed incompatible. Their languages were totally dissimilar, and their long-standing enmity was well known. It was probably a mistake to bring them together at the same mission.

since the lack of words in their language, and other words that they have not been able to understand to reconcile their languages with ours, makes it difficult to teach them more catechism. They pray in Spanish the Our Father, the Ave Maria, the Articles of Faith, and the *Salve*, and easily and in a short time they speak it so as to be understood.

We will place here a report of the status of the New California missions,[62] since it seems to us that it would not displease people who are interested in the well-being of their fellow men, and who, after having read the account of the progress of civilization on these coasts, are happy over the good outcome of the visits of the Spaniards to them, whatever may have been the object that motivated them, considering that there can't be omitted from these the happy results for its inhabitants, such as the cessation of many domestic wars that were destroying them, the moderation of their perpetual ill will, social beginnings, the acquisition of a religion that leads us to our true happiness by paths of pure love, and the knowledge of the means of gaining a more comfortable way of life than that of the animals, from which the Californians had scarcely emerged at the time of our first inquiries.

Departure of the schooners from Monterey. Because of bad weather, they miss exploring the coast until getting as far south as the Santa Barbara Channel. They explore the islands that form it, with the Mexicana *passing to the north of them and the* Sutil *to the south. They enter the port of San Diego, where they see the corvette* Concepción[63] *at anchor. They follow the coast as far as 27° 30' north latitude and leave it to explore the Farallones de los Alixos.[64] The currents push them leeward. They arrive at Cape San Lucas. They reunite with the* Concepción *and sight the Marías*

---

[62] This mission status report, including the page of text on the verso side, at some time became separated from the remainder of manuscript 1060. The single sheet was found bound into a volume of documents, appropriately entitled Miscelánea, which is number 2420 in the Museo Naval. The page is folio 87 of that particular volume. The report is reproduced below on pp. 158 and 160–61.

[63] The *Concepción*, under Lieutenant Francisco de Eliza, was listed as a frigate rather than a corvette. It had been built in the port of Realejo, Nicaragua, in 1788 and was 400 tons.

[64] The Farallones, now called Rocas Alijos, are located in 24° 58' north latitude and 115° 49' west longitude, well off the west coast of the Baja California peninsula.

Spanish Language	Eslen	Runsien	[English]
Q.: Quantos dioses hay?	Conumú dios?	Infan dios?	[How many gods are there?]
A.: Un solo Dios verdadero.	Pehe efes Dios sinuqui alapas patey.	Ynjala Dios ajlust yachaá.	[A single true God.]
Q.: Donde está Dios?	Quehaen Dios?	Antavar Dios?	[Where is God?]
A.: En el cielo, en la tierra y todas las cosas.	Ot no matsano comminam hecegui chaa.	Tarras turract in meitacast.	[In heaven, on the earth, and in everything.]
Q.: Quien hizo el cielo, la tierra y todas las cosas?	Quiniac heciha ot nomadsano comminan hecgui chaa?	Amp gisies imp tarrus Turract inmei intaguaya?	[Who made heaven, the earth and everything?]
A.: Dios nuestro Señor.	Dios Lechgpoio patama.	Dios mac Yayasamc.	[God our Lord.]
Q.: Quien es Dios Nuestro Señor?	Quiniac Dios?	Ampnui nesima Dios Mayayaramc?	[Who is God our Lord?]
A.: La Santisima Trinidad.	La Santisima Trinidad.	La Santisima Trinidad.	[The Holy Trinity.]
Q.: Quien es la Santisima Trinidad?	Quiniac Santisima Trinidad?	Ampnui Santisima Trinidad?	[Who is the Holy Trinity?]
A.: Dios Padre, Dios hijo, y Dios Espiritu Santo, personas distintas y un solo Dios verdadero.	Dios Lasayam, Dios Daspam, Dios Espiritu santo sulef personas gemelqua pehe Dios simiquiejes.	Dios appam, Dios insini, Dios espiritu santo capes personas sinaia injala alust Dios yachaa.	[God the Father, God the Son, and God the Holy Spirit, distinct persons and a single true God.]
Q.: El Padre es Dios?	Ca Dios ahic Lasayan?	Moc Appam Dios?	[Is the Father God?]
A.: Si, Dios verdadero.	Yque Dios efes.	Eeyachaa.	[Yes, true God.]
Q.: El hijo es Dios?	Ca Dios ahic Laspam?	Moc Ynsis Dios?	[Is the Son God?]
A.: Si, Dios verdadero.	Yque Dios efes.	Eeyachaa.	[Yes, true God.]
Q.: El espiritu Santo es Dios?	Ca Dios ahic Espiritu Santo?	Moc Espiritu Santo Dios?	[Is the Holy Spirit God?]
A.: Si, Dios verdadero.	Yque Dios efes.	Eeyachaa.	[Yes, true God.]

Spanish Language	Eslen	Runsien	[English]
Q.: Son tres Dioses estas tres personas?	Cajulet guahic Dios anniqua julef Personas?	Nesina capes Personas mocapes Dios?	[Are the three persons three Gods?]
A.: No son tres Dioses estas tres personas, un mismo ser tienen estas tres personas, por esto no tres Dioses son sino un solo Dios verdadero.	Maali sulef hua Dios anniqua julef Personas pehcalam pehcmatt sano la mohco anniqua julef Personas lali malilam julef hua Dios pehc Dios sui nuqui efes amohco.	Cuhue capes Dios nesinac Pes Personas, utieia huacaia imjala ajlust Dios Yachaa.	[These three persons are not three Gods. These three persons have a single being, therefore they are not three Gods, but a single true God.]
Q.: Qual se hizo hombre de estas tres personas?	Quiniac espia eggenoch anniqua julef Personas?	Yntau utf mocosim muquianc nisima capes Personas?	[Which of these three persons was made man?]
A.: El hijo, el qual llamamos Jesucristo.	Laspanna espia egge noch namo es legtos lepmus Jesucristo.	Hua Ynsus mocosim muquianc nisima tancurraque Jesu-cristo.	[The Son, which we call Jesus Christ.]
Q.: Quien es Jesucristo?	Quiniac Jesu-cristo?	Anpnui Jesu-cristo?	[Who is Jesus Christ?]
A.: Dios verdadero y hombre verdadero	Dios efes eggenoch efes chaa.	Huacaia ya chaá Dios ya chaa Muquianc	[True God and true man.]
Q.: Donde se hizo hombre el hijo de Dios?	Quegá espiaquiegge noch Dios Larpanna?	Annia utfs mocosim muquianc Dios Ynsis?	[Where was the Son of God made man?]
A.: En el vientre de una Muger llamada Santa Maria, por obra del Espiritu Santo. La Muger Santa Maria siempre fué virgen antes del parto, en el parto, y despues del parto.	Lauya las sigihania anniqui pec Lacta Santa Maria lamhoco toyoqul lalhalic jalama ijamis nemulam opssiame chaa.	Juyai pititataúna la chiamc Santa Maria huacaya sa gisie simp Espiritu Santo roteinia y impayomb yachaa Dios amp.	[In the womb of a woman named Saint Mary, by agency of the Holy Spirit. The woman Saint Mary was always a virgin, before, during, and after the birth.]
Q.: Por que se hizo hombre el hijo de Dios?	Casquiac espia egge noch Dios Laspanna?	Intamson mocosino Dios Ynsins?	[Why was the Son of God made man?]
A.: Para limpiar nuestras almas de nuestros pecados, y despues llevarnos al Cielo.	Hequepa legmasa neg anniquita legpachpa mamoesam lechú huchupmutsono.	Escomaques gichigua sirremaque quechens escomajes vattes Tarrajta.	[To cleanse our souls of our sins, and later to take us to Heaven.]

Spanish Language	Eslen	Runsien	[English]
Q.: Que hizo Jesu-cristo aquí en la tierra para lim-piar nuestras almas y llevarnos al Cielo?	Pasiac Lasipaya Jesucristo laimat-sanai hequepa lechisleg masa-negnamo es lechis huchupmus otno?	Yntas mur guisi tu-rrate maques gi-chigua sirrecusa maques huattes trrajta?	[What did Jesus Christ do here on earth to cleanse our souls and to take us to Heaven?]
A.: Padeció por mandato de Pon-cio Pilato, lo cru-cificaron, lo ma-taron y lo enterra-ron. Baxó a los Infiernos. Tres dias estubo. Re-sucitó subió a los Cielos está sen-tado a la diestra de Dios padre todo poderoso o que todo lo puede.	Tamma cahalass te telpa Poncio Pi-lato cocjo y laluis Santa Cruz nan-quinamul, lach-mam efem panaci, laccas luchmat sanahi lamhoco julefaszt canay namulan foila eguepmus laca yajam ot no-jam cosontalpaya Dios Lasacion comminam iquipa.	Huijais tisimp hua-cainc ihasim Pon-cio Pilato, cusa pajan juay Santa Cruz lacust pi-rastuchap piquini huinumb capes tuujs pusep simp-jop pequini turr-jat pinaisi juya tavar samatc Dios Apaninmu a tu mam.	[He suffered by order of Pontius Pilate, they cru-cified him, killed him, and buried him. He de-scended into Hell. He was there for three days. Resur-rected, he as-cended into Heaven. He is seated at the right hand of God the Father all-powerful, or who can do everything.]
Q.: Quando murió Jesucristo en la cruz murió en quanto Dios o en quanto hombre?	Vmases chuncaimos Jesucristo la huis Santa Cruz ca-chunaimos ques-chunas hi haias Dios caeggenoch tibac chunas hihaia?	Tanamur lacué ja ya Santa Cruz Jesu-cristo nocmur Dios jacunsin as-smaqui anc?	[When Jesus Christ died on the cross did he die as God or as man?]
A.: No murió en quanto Dios sino en quanto hombre.	Maalilam chuna si-ame Dios eg-genoch alagua teipas chu-nasiame.	Cuve maur Dios la cansim exemux muquianc lacunsin.	[He didn't die as God but as man.]
Q.: Y el hombre quando muere, muere en quanto al alma o en quanto al cuerpo?	Vamases chunaimos efege cachuna igmus ques las masaneg cala saques mepgel alagua teipas chanaimus ú?	Ymanu lacun mu-quiane mocsirre lacun asturrumb lacum?	[When man dies, does his soul die or only his body?]
A.: No muere en quanto al alma sino en quanto al cuerpo.	Maalilam chunai-mus halassmaasa negmepgel sinnu chunaimurha.	Cuve lacum sirre enea turrumb lacum.	[He doesn't die in his soul but only his body.]

Spanish Language	Eslen	Runsien	[English]
Q.: Y el cuerpo del hombre muere para siempre?	Camepgel lic chun aimus há eguaimitans?	Turrumb mu-quiancmocs haim lacum?	[And does the body of a man die forever?]
A.: No por que el dia del juicio se tornaran a juntar las almas con sus mismos cuerpos y asi resucitarán para nunca mas morir.	Malilam chunai-musa egua imi-tand susqui asatsani teipa imitaniti namoes lach tivijap mas-aneg alalu lags mepgel namoes achepal namoeses alic chunaical.	Cuve incat tanayi yitujs imach catuque pirre, casacu mac muche pmac sirre sturrumb cuse-mac tanay pusep es comac cuve ataplacum.	[No, because on Judgment Day all souls will be united again with their own bodies and will be thus resurrected never to die again.]
Q.: A donde van las almas de los bue-nos Cristianos quando mueren sus cuerpos?	Que es temujus aimasaneg anni-qua salequa chris-tianos umases lachs chumaimus mejojel?	Annuatim asirre nusina misgin-cai cristianos imano lacum batarrumb?	[Where do the souls of good Chris-tians go when their bodies die?]
A.: Al cielo a gozar de Dios para siempre por que obedecieron los mandamientos.	Nasi otno gilagila panai egua imi-tans iyual gicya Dios nes alavis cadsquiolospa lachslaste telpa Dios nisa.	Juya tarrajta siunite Dios escoaim pa huicat vamai is-tap Dios ranips.	[To Heaven to en-joy God forever because they obeyed his commandments.]
Q.: A donde van las almas de los malos Cristianos quando mueren sus cuerpos?	Que es tupjumus masaneg aniquas pachqua cris-tianos umases lachs chunaimus mepgel?	An huatim vasirre nisina que chiem cai imanu lacum vaturrumb?	[Where do the souls of bad Christians go when their bodies die?]
A.: Al Infierno a padecer para siempre por que no obedecieron los mandamien-tos de Dios.	Lavis madsano luch madsanai, tama-cusuja egua im-itans iyual cadsquimaalilam oloipa Dios misa tetelpa.	Juya huniump iyai vijaitin aipirrey incat ninc mur mayigin Dios nips.	[To Hell to suffer forever because they did not obey God's command-ments.]
Q.: Que es la Santa Iglesia?	Quet seaia Santa Iglesia?	Amp Santa Iglesia?	[What is the Holy Church?]
A.: Es una con-gregacion de los Cristianos que creen lo que dice Dios y obedecen al Papa.	Pectin impa anni qua cristianos Mechja Dios mical Paoloipa lachs Papanis cháa.	Muchep piquini yo Cristianos maiacs nip Dios unque sac Papa.	[It is a congregation of Christians who believe what God says and who obey the Pope.]

Spanish Language	Eslen	Runsien	[English]
Q.: Quien está en el Santisimo Sacramento del altar?	Quiniac occopu lasi Santisimo Sacramento del altar?	Amp juyat Santisimo Sacramento del altar?	[Who is in the Most Holy Sacrament of the altar?]
A.: Jesu Cristo nuestro Señor y hombre verdadero.	Jesucristo Lechs poyo patan Dios efes eggenohes efes cháa.	Jesucristo mac Yayaran, yachaa Dios muquianc.	[Jesus Christ, our Lord and true man.]
Q.: Que debemos hacer para comulgar?	Pasiques sassipija tan momo comulgar?	Ymmadac comulgar intascumac gisih?	[What must we do to commune?]
A.: Llegar en ayunas y confesados si tuviesemos algun pecado mortal.	Hamo es legalic amma namo es legalic tateicala meguas sacap tumanis nomo es leg, confesar, japjatam umases taa coliquit pachspa.	Yilui uspigasa cumac confesar imad notei quechens.	[Arrive fasting and confessed if we have some mortal sin.]
Q.: Para confesarnos que debemos hacer?	Pasiques sasipi umases lechs confesar jap?	Ynmadac confesar intas cumac gisih?	[What must we do to confess?]
A.: Pensar antes nuestros pecados, despues decir al padre todos los grandes, sentir en nuestro corazon no haber obedecido los mandamientos de Dios, decir verdad en nuestras almas de no volver a decir pecados nunca.	Logma saja jatan lechija pachspa confesar jap comminam coliquit mantagqui maaca agua alpamantag qui alicta tei calleg pachspa.	Poeessoi ini iomac quee oquep Padre inmei cachmon sirre macguas tarmam pi simp maccarraa richiseza escomac cuve adap.	[Think first of our sins, then tell all the big ones to the priest; feel in our hearts that we haven't obeyed God's commandments, vow in our souls that we will not tell lies any more.]
Q.: Que hemos de hacer para ir al Cielo?	Pasiques sasipiu maies leg tempus otno?	Yntas comacgisc si inmadac Tarrajta huatiq?	[What do we have to do to go to Heaven?]
A.: Guardar los mandamientos de Dios, los de la Santa Madre Iglesia, y cumplir con las obligaciones de nuestro estado.	Tajauy lasstetel pa Dios chaas lasstetel palechsgadsia Santa Iglesia eguacas sipsa sipa.	Yannis saqnuma jsinaovest Dios maqaan Santa Iglesia huagise sien hai amagiscsien.	[Keep God's commandments, those of the Holy Mother Church, and comply with the obligations of our status.]
Amen Jesus	Amen Jesus	Amen Jesus	[Amen Jesus]

Islands. A strong squall hits them, with risk to the schooners. They finally anchor safely in the port of San Blas.

October 1792. We were ready on the 23d to set sail, but the wind shifted to the north and we couldn't do so. The frigate [*Santa*] *Gertrudis* was also about to leave for San Blas, and on it we sent to the viceroy of New Spain the finished map and an extract of our explorations.[65] On the 25th the wind calmed, and at 2:00 A.M. on the 26th we weighed anchor, leaving in port the aforementioned frigate.

At dawn we had already passed Point of Pines, but the SE wind that blew with strength and cloudbursts during the day was adverse for our following the coast, and it carried us away from it so that we were not able to see it at sunset. The night continued squally, and at 1:30 there was a heavy shower and downpour, with which the SE wind slackened and a clearing opened to the northwest, giving indication of wind from that direction. It was not slow in happening, and we had fair weather all of the 27th, taking advantage of it on our course to the Santa Barbara Channel.

This channel formed by the coast and a chain of islands needed to be examined. The commander of the expedition of the corvettes *Descubierta* and *Atrevida* [Malaspina] had given to some points on the first islands a position so different from that which they had on the map that the pilots of San Blas used for their navigation in that area that the direction of the channel could not be laid down without arbitrarily changing the location of the islands not seen by that commandant. Therefore we thought it necessary for us to make some effort to explore them. Don Juan [Francisco] de la Bodega [y Quadra] and the pilots of that area advised us to give up our plan, bearing in mind the nature of our vessels, the advanced season of the year, and the fact that there were not any ports for our protection from the south winds, which blow strongly and

---

[65] The reigning viceroy of New Spain, to whom the map and extract were sent, was Juan Vicente de Güemes Pacheco de Padilla, Conde de Revilla Gigedo. Besides acting as courier for the reports, the *Santa Gertrudis* departed from California carrying as a passenger Josefa Sandoval, widow of the recently deceased governor, José Antonio Roméu.

"Status of the Missions of New California . . . 1791" (*Estado de las Misiones de la Nueva California . . . 1791*). Report by Fermín Franciso de Lasuén, Vargas Ponce, MS 1060, Museo Naval.

"Status of the Missions of New California in the Years Indicated" (*Estado de las Misiones de la nueva California en los años que se expresa*). Report by Fermín Francisco de Lasuén, 1792, Vargas Ponce, MS 1060, Museo Naval.

with heavy black clouds. But we were too much influenced by the usefulness that would be produced from it to abandon the undertaking.

So on the 28th we headed for the channel, and at nightfall, since we were very close, it was decided that one schooner, the *Mexicana*, would pass to the north and the *Sutil* to the south of the islands. On the 29th at 10:30 A.M. we sighted the Farallones de Lobos: This day we coasted the islands of San Cleto [San Anacleto] and San Miguel.[66] Laying to at night with a very clear moon, we examined Santa Barbara Island, running a base line from it and taking the moon's meridian altitude on the same base line [to determine the latitude]. At dawn on the 31st we were off the northwest point of Santa Catalina Island. Here the schooners reunited and ran base lines along the south shore of this island, getting by afternoon as far as its southeastern part, where the extent of San Andrés Island[67] was determined geometrically. Since it was a long way off, precaution was taken for the exactness of bearings by using the sun, determining them without the compass by means of azimuths of that body and the vertical angle that it formed with the points of reference.

November 1792. We spent the night calmly, and at daybreak we were off San Andrés Island. During the day we had calm, light winds that didn't allow us to draw the details of the map of this island. The following day we had the same problem, but since they were a little more constant, we took advantage of them and sailed looking for the port of San Diego, having set down the position of all the islands, even though for that of San Nicolás[68] we only made

[66] San Cleto Island, also referred to as San Anacleto, had appeared as a place-name as early as the Vizcaíno expedition of 1602. Today it is called San Miguel Island. On other maps it has appeared as San Bernardo and as San Ambrosio. The San Miguel Island of 1792 is now called Santa Rosa Island, but at times was also designated as San Ambrosio. Santa Cruz Island, when and if mentioned, was always so called. Anacapa Island, frequently left unlabeled, was sometimes called Santo Tomás Island.

[67] San Andrés was what is today called San Clemente Island, the southernmost of the Channel Islands.

[68] San Nicolás is the Channel Island that lies farthest from the mainland. It was viewed at considerable distance in 1792, but a year earlier the corvettes *Descubierta*

Missions	Years	Indian inhabitants				Livestock		Plantings and Harvests	
								Wheat	
		Baptisms	Mar-riages	Deaths	Living	Major	Minor	Sown	Harvested
San Diego	1785	—	—	—	—	—	—	43	367
(latitude 32° 42')	1790	1,452	—	—	933	1,306	1,583	34	203
	1791	1,511	350	557	883	2,603	2,155	60	302
San Juan de	1785	—	—	—	—	—	—	37	80
Capistrano	1790	1,059	—	—	765	2,328	4,700	57	1,020
(latitude 33° 30')	1791	1,096	270	335	766	2,490	6,301	80	1,586
San Gabriel	1785	—	—	—	—	—	—	80	1,500
Archangel	1790	1,953	—	—	1,078	3,800	4,980	160	2,375
(latitude 34° 10')	1791	2,191	442	926	1,204	4,523	6,476	178	3,700
San Buenaventura	1785	—	—	—	—	—	—	3	31
(latitude 34° 20')	1790	534	—	—	419	771	965	22	155
	1791	642	111	151	462	996	1,224	44	259
Santa Barbara	1785	—	—	—	—	—	—	—	—
(latitude 34° 29')	1790	593	—	—	407	208	286	60	725
	1791	749	171	168	499	348	540	65	1,500
Purísima	1785	—	—	—	—	—	—	—	—
Concepción	1790	301	—	—	278	169	464	25	530
(latitude 34° 35')	1791	488	97	51	434	232	614	76	800
San Luis Obispo	1785	—	—	—	—	—	—	30	500
(latitude 35° 20')	1790	924	—	—	599	3,456	3,387	100	1,200
	1791	1,057	238	348	682	5,073	4,728	86	1,078
San Antonio de	1785	—	—	—	—	—	—	44	1,000
Padua	1790	1,771	—	—	1,092	2,000	1,660	110	690
(latitude 36° 30')	1791	1,844	265	761	1,083	2,400	1,353	90	952
San Carlos	1785	—	—	—	—	—	—	24	89
(latitude 36° 30')	1790	1,550	—	—	712	1,082	900	69	692
	1791	1,693	432	845	770	1,193	1,146	71	221
Santa Clara	1785	—	—	—	—	—	—	22	200
(latitude 37°)	1790	1,972	—	—	940	3,080	800	32	1,030
	1791	2,006	245	987	957	3,000	828	64	1,400
Our Holy Father	1785	—	—	—	—	—	—	18	175
San Francisco	1790	904	—	—	525	1,800	1,700	42½	538
(latitude 37° 56')	1791	1,031	251	395	590	2,000	2,010	60	680

NOTE: All measurements are in fanegas or parts of fanegas. A fanega is a hundredweight. An almud ("al.") is half a fanega, or a little more than eight pounds.

Plantings and Harvests

Barley		Corn		Beans		Chickpeas		Lentils		Peas		Horsebeans	
Sown	Harvested	Sown	Harvested	Sown	Harvested	Sown	Harvested	Sown	Harvested	Sown	Harvested	Sown	Harvested
13	70	—	—	1⅓	0	—	—	—	—	—	—	—	—
12½	900	1½	50	5	6	—	—	—	—	—	—	—	—
16	1,437	9	52	2	50	—	—	—	—	—	—	—	—
—	—	6	900	3	130	—	—	—	—	—	—	—	—
—	—	6	1,030	2	27	—	—	—	—	—	—	—	—
2	52	10.1	1,854	3.1	136	—	—	—	—	—	—	—	—
—	—	11	1,000	6	201	6/25	18	1	5	—	—	—	—
—	—	13	1,600	6	110	⅓	12	—	2	—	—	—	—
—	—	16	1,680	7	246	8	4	½ al.	2	—	—	—	—
6/25	5	2	511	4	33	6/25	7	3/25	6	—	—	6	5
18	719	9	1,000	18	167	4/25	10/25	—	—	—	—	2	9
—	—	9.3	1,600	6	90	10	0	—	—	—	—	2	3
6	100	1½	50	5	60	1	3	—	—	—	—	—	—
8	340	2½	262	6	118	½	1	—	—	—	—	4	½
½	16	3	251	4	70	—	—	—	—	1/25	2	—	—
—	—	3.1	653	3½	131	3	0	—	—	2½	2	—	—
—	—	8/25	3	6	1½/25	—	—	—	—	—	—	—	—
—	—	2	75	½	1	—	—	—	—	1/25	1	1	2
—	—	2½	123	2	33½	—	—	1	6	—	—	—	—
—	—	4	464	4	0	—	—	—	—	—	—	—	—
6	27	7	108	3	25	—	—	—	—	1	6	6/25	2
5	72	3	151	2	21	—	—	—	—	10	6.1	2	2
33	350	5½	160	5	85	—	—	—	—	2	2	2	1
62½	675	11	820	10	145	—	—	1	7	4	101	3	13
52	536	11	150	13½	211	—	—	1½	9	4	110	3	40
—	—	6	260	6	18	1	9	1	4½	1	9	1	4
—	—	8½	600	7	60	2	3	1	5	1	9	1	9/25
—	—	10	900	6½	74	2	14	3	4	1	13	1	0
17	458	1	55	2	6	6/25	—	6/25	1¼	6/25	4¼	1	18
38	439	6½	367	12	38	—	—	1½	12	3	30	9	68
34	506	10	200	10	90	—	—	1	17	2	52	6	55

a note that it had already been set down the previous year. These islands are of a moderate elevation and do not have trees. Of them only Santa Catalina provides two ports in the midst of its two coasts, northeast and southwest. Dividing them is a low, narrow tongue of land. The aspect of the horizon made us fear a change in the good weather that had favored us the previous days. During the night we kept in sight of the coast. There a strong squall hit us with a SW wind and much rain, but it slackened in a short while, and by dawn it was mild. The wind settled to the west, the sky cleared, and we headed for the Point of San Diego, the longitude and latitude of which we tried to determine. We passed close by it sounding from above the seaweed and giving a wide berth to the shoal that projects southward. As soon as we doubled it, we sighted the corvette *Concepción,* which we had left at Nootka upon our departure to reconnoiter [the Strait of Juan de] Fuca. A canoe set out from it with Ensign Don Juan Matute,[69] who told us that the corvette was detained because of a lack of provisions for its voyage to San Blas, for which it was making ready.

We entered the bay staying close to the west shore, giving a wide berth to the shoals that are located on the east shore, which jut out almost halfway across and make entrance to the port difficult.[70] It was our purpose to be at noon at the parallel of the Point of San Diego to determine its latitude, and once near the entrance

---

and *Atrevida* had passed close enough to chart its coordinates. Of all the Channel Islands, it was the one that was placed most inaccurately on the map used by the San Blas pilots.

[69] Juan Matute y Corres was a career naval officer. In the following year, 1793, he made an exploration of Tomales Bay (then called Bodega Bay) as a preliminary step to possible Spanish occupation aimed at thwarting rumored Russian interest in that area. Matute's meeting off San Diego with Dionisio Alcalá Galiano brought together two future martyrs of the famous Battle of Trafalgar, the last and bloodiest battle of the "age of sail." Alcalá Galiano died commanding the *Bahama,* and Matute lost his life aboard the *Trinidad.* British success brought fame to Admiral Nelson and gave London a cherished landmark and monument to that engagement at Trafalgar Square.

[70] These shoals appear on the San Blas pilots' map of the period as the Bajos de Zúñiga.

we veered and carried out with full satisfaction the observation of the sun's meridian altitude.

We continued our navigation with favorable weather for passing between the Coronados [Islands] and the coast and for drawing the map of the portion of it between the Point of San Diego and 32° 10' latitude.

Since our operations were not to have been dedicated to anything more than mapping the coast, and since this was already competently set in position, following a straight course and working as the day permitted, we continued our operations in this way. On the 4th we covered the area between 31° 35' and 31° 20' latitude; on the 5th, between 30° 30' and 29° 45'; on the 6th, that portion of the Gulf of Cerros[71] from 15° 45' to 14° 25' longitude [west of San Blas]; and on the 7th we continued by the Isle of Cerros[72] along the channel formed by the Isla de Trinidad[73] and the coast, ending this day in 27° 30' latitude in a bay with a good anchoring ground of sand, which could be the port of San Bartolomé,[74] so named by Sebastián Vizcaíno.

We would have followed the coast as far as Cape San Lucas if another more interesting point had not called our attention. The maps of the San Blas department pilots place some rocky islands called Los Alixos in 24° latitude, but the frigate *San Andrés* of the Philippine trade, in its navigation from there to Acapulco in 1792, said that it had observed their location in a latitue of 23° 34' [changed to 24° 34'] with a certainty and a detail of their activities that obliged the commander of the corvettes *Descubierta* and *Atrevida* [Malaspina] to accept it and to place on his map this latter position as preferable. The pilots said that theirs was certain, and

[71] The Gulf of Cerros is today called the Bahía de Sebastián Vizcaíno.

[72] The Isle of Cerros appears on many maps as Isla de Cedros, the largest offshore island on the coast of the Californias.

[73] The Isla de Trinidad in this context was probably the Isla de Natividad which appears on both the Vizcaíno maps and those of the voyage of the *Sutil* and *Mexicana*.

[74] Vizcaíno's Puerto de San Bartolomé became a brief stop for the *Sutil* and *Mexicana*. Today it appears on maps as Bahía San Bartolomé and sometimes as Bahía Tortugas.

seeing their diaries and the strong reasons upon which their opinions were founded, it seemed to be a matter worthy of our occupying ourselves with its solution.[75]

Consequently, we set our course to hit that parallel at 20 leagues west of those shoals, where we arrived at 4:00 P.M. on the 9th. At that point a second separation of the schooners was decided, with the *Mexicana* running the parallel of 24° 26' [changed to 24° 56'] and the *Sutil* that of 24° 30', thus leaving an interval of 36 [*sic*] miles, and [with us] hoping to examine closely in this way all parallels in which the Alixos could be. With our clocks synchronized, we set as our point of reunion 24° 30' latitude and 15° longitude.

But what was our surprise on finding ourselves, according to our noon observation, having lost ten minutes to southward, considering that, by the tacking at night with the mainsails, we had done nothing more than maintain ourselves, and since on the preceding days we had experienced no current! Realizing the loss, the *Sutil* began to make headway under full sail against the wind. But the next day we found ourselves in 24° 22', having lost 40' in addition to the 21' set to windward according to our reckoning.

The *Mexicana*, which had the same loss, fell to 24° latitude [changed to 24° 30'], and since its efforts to regain its parallel were useless, its commander [Valdés] decided to explore that of the *Sutil*, figuring that this vessel would have been overcome by a similar fate. As a result, in this way the parallel of 24° 34' would be inspected to complete satisfaction, with the *Mexicana* sailing along 24° 38' and the *Sutil* along very nearly 24° 30'. On the 12th at 2:00 A.M. the schooners reunited at the given latitude and longitude. In these events the poor characteristics of the vessels were also an obstacle, but we were able to give assurance that the Alixos were not in the position given for them by the frigate *San Andrés*, nor within twenty minutes of it, and therefore that the

[75] The commanding officer of the nao *San Andrés* in 1791 was Naval Lieutenant Joaquín de Marquina. A revised calculation based on Marquina's observation of October 31, 1791, made by José Espinosa several years after the event, placed the elusive Alijos in 24° 46' 30".

position of the pilots was the correct one.[76] The corvette *Concepción,* which left from the port of San Diego and headed for them, sighted them and verified the latitude and longitude as that in which they were formerly set down.

Once the schooners were reunited they set a course for Cape San Lucas. The wind followed them fresh from WNW, and the weather was clear; and thus at dawn on the 15th the coast of the extreme south of the peninsula of the Californias was seen, and at noon we were in the meridian of that cape. We marked off a base line, we made one-hour runs, and we found that the Arnold chronometer number 344 gave a difference of 13 minutes less longitude between this cape and Monterey than that determined by the corvettes the year before. Since during the cruise we had been able to get little good out of chronometer number 16, we relied on the results of a single chronometer, to which, because of many better previous results, we corrected our intermediate latitudes under the supposition of an error of arithmetic progression, which conjecture we found verified in the checking of its movement.

Before arriving at our port of destination, we still had to examine the Islas Marías and Isabela.[77] There was some disagreement about their position, with the pilots of the department of San Blas giving reasons against the placement of them according to the commander of the expedition of the corvettes *Descubierta* and *Atrevida,* and so we had to verify those points. Three days of good wind were sufficient for our purposes, but on crossing the mouth of the Sea of Cortés,[78] we had calms and mild weather and we commenced to make but little distance. On the 18th we sighted a vessel on the west, and at noon it joined up with us. It was the corvette *Concepción,* commanded by Lieutenant Francisco Elisa,

---

[76] None of the positions was very accurate.

[77] The Islas Marías, frequently called the Tres Marías, are, from northwest to southeast, María Madre, María Magdalena, and María Cleofas. They lie almost due west of San Blas and some fifty to seventy miles offshore. Isla Isabela lies some fifteen miles offshore directly northwest of San Blas and therefore east-northeast of the Islas Marías.

[78] The mouth of the Gulf of California.

who did us the favor of convoying us, shortening sail because of the great speed advantage he had over us. We continued in convoy, taking advantage of the fair winds, which, upon becoming fresh on the afternoon of the 20th, permitted us at nightfall from the crow's nest of the *Concepción* to see the most northwesterly of those islands.

On the 21st we were off them at daybreak. The latitude of the most northerly part was observed, but we couldn't continue to map it because we were overcome by calms. At nightfall they continued, and the sky was squally. The currents dragged us to the southeast, headed for the narrow strait [79] formed by the two most northerly Marías Islands.

At 1:00 A.M. a squall came upon us which exposed us to considerable danger. It started from the north and ran to the west. Such was the gust of wind that, although it only caught the *Mexicana* in the pocket of the mainsail, it almost capsized her. The *Sutil* followed behind with sails lowered, but what caused greater concern to both was, owing to the great amount of water and wind, the binnacle lamp was extinguished, one of the principal causes being that the glass was broken. The spare lantern that was kept for such accidents was brought out, and it also went out, so the schooners were left without knowing in which direction they were heading. We longed for the consolation of the brightness of the lightning flashes in order to see the needle and to keep ourselves away from the islands and from the corvette *Concepción*. The squall abated while we were drawing away from the former, and we returned to the tranquility that favorable seas provide. But the schooners didn't see each other again all night, this being the first time they had parted company except for the two nights when they had done so on purpose; for despite the little advantage that great care and union offered, separation had been avoided.

At dawn the two schooners reunited, and the commander of the *Concepción* was asked if he would bend all efforts possible to make

---

[79] Both here and elsewhere the journal writer used the Catalan word *freu* for a narrow strait—perhaps because the chief of charts and maps of the Malaspina expedition was a Catalan-speaker, Felipe Bauzá.

port, since no advantage came from the delay he was suffering. As a result of this suggestion, he set full sail and headed off. After taking bearings of the Marías Islands, we set sail for that of Isabela to continue our work. The squally weather and the gusty wind prevented our work from having the accuracy that we desired. Although we could not observe a noon latitude, that calculated by two solar altitudes proved to us how much we had been pulled southward by the currents. In the afternoon the wind freshened from the southeast, the sky cleared somewhat, we sighted Isabela, and we headed for it. We ran a base and took bearings at the same time on the Marías and on the Cerro de San Juan.[80]

At nightfall it was squally, and the *Concepción* was in sight. During the night, after a cloudburst with considerable wind and water, the sky cleared, the wind shifted to the northwest, and we headed in search of the white rock that is used as a landmark for the port of San Blas.[81] At dawn it was in sight, and the *Concepción* was a great distance astern. At 11:00 A.M. we anchored, finding there the war frigate *Gertrudis* and the corvette *San José de las Animas,* which had arrived from Manila under the command of Lieutenant Manuel Quimper.[82]

Our crews arrived in the best of health and with the greatest joy, receiving the congratulations of their friends on seeing them free from such dangerous and laborious navigation, during which they had given proof of subordination and perseverance worthy of the greatest praise.

[80] Cerro de San Juan was a prominent landmark some twenty miles east of the harbor at San Blas. It was quite visible from the sea under normal conditions.

[81] The offshore white rock (Piedra Blanca) still serves as a prominent landmark near the San Blas harbor entrance.

[82] Manuel Quimper was a familiar figure on the Pacific Coast. In 1790, as commanding officer of the Frigate *Princesa,* he had explored the Strait of Juan de Fuca as a precursor of the *Sutil* and *Mexicana* visitors. In 1791, Quimper became the first official Spanish visitor to Hawaii. At that time he was returning to San Blas from the extension of a trip that had taken him to the Philippine Islands.

Bibliography

Manuscripts

Archivo General de Indias (AGI), Sevilla.
  Audiencia de Guadalajara 493, 494.
  Audiencia de México 1523, 1545, 1548, 1563.
Archivo General de la Nación (AGN), Mexico City.
  Historia 558.
  Marina 73, 82, 92.
Archivo General Militar, Segovia.
  Expediente matrimonial—José Cardero.
Archivo Histórico Nacional (AHN), Madrid.
  Papeles de Estado 4287, 4288, 4290.
Archivo de la Iglesia de Santa María y Santa Bárbara, Ecija.
  Libro de Bautismo 26.
Archivo del Ministerio de Asuntos Exteriores (AMAE), Madrid.
  Manuscripts 13, 146.
Archivo-Museo Don Alvaro de Bazán (AMAB), El Viso del Marqués.
  Asuntos personales de Alcalá Galiano, Cardero, Salamanca, Valdés, and Vernacci.
Museo de América, Madrid.
Museo Naval (MN), Madrid.
  Corbetas, tomo 6, MS 95.
  Viaje al Estrecho de Fuca, tomo 2, MS 144.
  Viage en Limpio de las Corbetas Descubierta y Atrevida, MS 181.
  Diarios, tomo 6, MS 276.
  Malaspina Correspondencia, tomos 1–3, MSS 278, 279, 280.

California y Costa N.O. de America, tomo 1, MS 330.

Reino de México, tomo 3, MS 335.

Apuntes, noticias y correspondencia pertenecientes a la espedición de Malaspina, MS 427.

Correspondencia relativa al viage de Malaspina, MS 583.

Malaspina, Descripción de California, MS 621.

Notas del Don Francisco Mourelle, MS 999.

Vargas Ponce, MS 1060.

Lista de los oficiales agregados a la compañía de Guardias Marinas: Año de 1792, MS 1099.

Lista de los oficiales agregados a la compañía de Guardias Marinas: Año de 1794, MS 1100.

Libro de Oficiales agregados . . . para estudios mayores . . . , MS 1146.

Historial de los servicios de los Capitanes generales que tubo la armada, MS 1193.

Oficiales 1821–1836, MS 1251.

Fallecidos 1809–1824, MS 1256.

Malaspina Pintores, 1788–1795, MS 1827.

Miscelánea, 1394–1874, MS 2110.

Malaspina Expedición Pintores, 1789–1798, MS 2219.

Malaspina, 1788–1814, MS 2296.

Miscelánea, 1610–1881, MS 2420.

San Blas pilots map, signature IV-B-7 in map collection.

Published Sources

Acalá Galiano, Dionisio. *Memoria sobre el cálculo de la latitud del lugar por dos alturas del sol.* Madrid, 1795.

———. *Memoria sobre de las observaciones de latitud y longitud en el mar.* Madrid, 1796.

Archibald, Robert. *The Economic Aspects of the California Missions.* Washington, D.C., 1978.

Atlas para el viage de las goletas Sutil y Mexicana. Madrid. 1802.

Beals, Herbert K. *For Honor and Country: The Diary of Bruno de Hezeta.* Portland, 1985.

Bancroft, Hubert H. *History of California.* Vol. 1 of seven vols. San Francisco, 1884–90.

Berrocal Garrido, José A. *El Panteón de Ilustres Marinos.* Cádiz, 1890.

Boorstin, Daniel J. *The Discoverers.* New York, 1983.

Cutter, Donald C. "California, Training Ground for Spanish Naval Heroes." California Historical Society Quarterly 40, no. 2 (June, 1961).

———. Malaspina in California. San Francisco, 1960.

———. "Pedro de Alberni y los primeros experimentos de agricultura científica en la costa noroeste del Pacífico." Revista de Historia Naval 5 (1987), no. 18.

———. "The Return of Malaspina," The American West, 15, no. 1 (January–February 1978).

———. "Spanish Exploration of California's Central Valley." Ph.D. dissertation, University of California, Berkeley, 1950.

———, ed. and trans. Journal of Tomás de Suría of His Voyage with Malaspina to the Northwest Coast of America in 1791. Fairfield, Wash., 1980.

Destefani, Laurio, and Donald Cutter. Tadeo Haenke y el final de una vieja polémica. Buenos Aires, 1966.

[Engstrand], Iris Wilson, ed. Noticias de Nutka. Seattle, 1970.

Engstrand, Iris H. W. Spanish Scientists in the New World. Seattle, 1981.

Espinosa, Josef de. Memoria sobre las observaciones astronómicas . . . Madrid, 1805.

Geiger, Maynard. Franciscan Missionaries in Hispanic California. San Marino, 1969.

Guest, Francis F. Fermín Francisco de Lasuén (1736–1803): A Biography. Washington, D.C., 1973.

Heizer, Robert F. "The Introduction of Monterey Shells to the Indians of the Northwest Coast." Pacific Northwest Quarterly 31 (1940), no. 4.

———, ed. California. Volume 8 of Handbook of North American Indians. Washington, D.C., 1978.

Jane, Lionel Cecil, ed. A Spanish Voyage to Vancouver and the Northwest Coast of America. London, 1930.

Kendrick, John. "The Brig Sutil—Its Hull, Rig and Equipment." Typescript report, 1987 (in Vancouver Maritime Museum, British Columbia).

Kenneally, Finbar, trans. and ed. The Writings of Fermín Francisco de Lasuén. 2 vols. Washington, D.C., 1965.

Kroeber, Alfred L. Handbook of the Indians of California. Washington, D.C., 1925.

Mathes, W. Michael. *Vizcaíno and Spanish Expansion in the Pacific Ocean, 1580–1630.* San Francisco, 1968.

Moorhead, Max L. *The Presidio: Bastion of the Spanish Borderlands.* Norman, 1975.

Novo y Colson, Pedro de, ed. *Viaje político-científico alrededor del mundo por las corbetas Descubierta y Atrevida, al mando de los capitanes de navío Don Alejandro Malaspina y Don José Bustamante y Guerra desde 1789 a 1794.* Madrid, 1885.

Pavia, Francisco de Paula. *Galería Biográfica de los Generales de Marina.* 4 vols. Madrid, 1873–74.

Relación del viage hecho por las goletas Sutil y Mexicana en el año de 1792. . . . 2 vols. Madrid, 1802.

Salvá, Jaime. *Alcalá Galiano.* Cartagena, no date.

Servin, Manuel P. "The Quest for the Governorship of Spanish California." *California Historical Society Quarterly* 43, no. 1 (March 1964).

Sotos Serrano, Carmen. *Los Pintores de la expedición de Alejandro Malaspina.* 2 vols. Madrid, 1982.

Thurman, Michael E. *The Naval Department of San Blas: New Spain's Bastion for Alta California and Nootka Sound, 1767–1798.* Glendale, 1967.

Venegas, Miguel. *Noticia de la California.* 3 vols. Madrid, 1757.

Wagner, Henry R. *Spanish Explorations in the Strait of Juan de Fuca.* Santa Ana, Calif., 1933.

Index

Acapulco: 6, 44ff; 63
Activa (Spanish vessel): 88, 90, 111,
   111n
Alberni, Pedro: 37, 38, 38n
Alcalá Galiano, Dionisio: 3, 5ff; in
   battle of Trafalgar, 51, 64; biogra-
   phy, 55–61; obtains catechism of
   Indians, 87; journal of his expedi-
   tion, 103–67
Alijos, Los (Rocas Alijos): 97, 98, 150;
   search for, 163–65
Anian, Strait of: 4, 5, 49
Aránzazu (frigate): 109, 109n, 111,
   112
Archivo General de Indias, Seville: 44
Arenaza, Father Pascual Martínez de
   (Franciscan): 82, 84–85, 94, 129n
Argüello, José Dario: 30, 35, 36, 47,
   82, 84, 94, 121n; commended by
   Malaspina, 41–42; biography, 84
Arrillaga, José Joaquin, 36, 41
Atrevida: see Descubierta and Atrevida

Bahama (Spanish warship): 58, 59
Barceló, Antonio: 50
Bauzá, Felipe: 71, 166n
Bodega y Quadra, Juan Francisco de la:
   19, 88, 89, 106, 107, 119, 158; and
   Expedition of the Limits, 73, 93

Bonaventura, Rio de: 46
Borica, Diego de: 40–41
Brambila, Fernando: 68
Branciforte, Marqués de: 85
Branciforte, Villa de: 38
Brand, John: 92–94
Brest, France: 51, 62, 77
Bustamante y Guerra, José: 4, 87; see
   also Descubierta and Atrevida

Caamaño, Jacinto: 111, 111n
Cádiz: 20, 25ff; Junta de, 52, 78;
   Naval Department of, 72, 75, 77
California, economy of: 31, 117; popu-
   lation, 28; agriculture, 32–35; fur
   trade, 43–45; abalone, 118; whales,
   119; status of missions, 156–59
California, military status of: 121–28
Cañizares, José: 45
Carlos IV: 72
Carmelo: river, 31, 82, 128; mission,
   149
Carrasco, Juan: 6, 69
Casa Tilly, Marqués: 55
Catalonian Volunteers: 37, 81
Catechism of Rumsen and Esselen In-
   dians: 151–55
Cazador (ship): 51, 70
Ceballos, Pedro de: 55

Central Valley, exploration: 46
Cepeda, Felix: 93, 94
Channel Islands, 17, 95, 97
Chumash Indians, basketry: 88
Columbia River: 17, 109; see also
    Hezeta Entrance
Concepción (naval vessel): 80, 150, 162,
    165–67
Cook, James: 20, 107 n, 112
Córdoba, Antonio de: 56
Córdoba, José de: 51
Córdoba, Luis de: 50
Coronados Islands: 163
Cortés, Sea of: 165

Descubierta and Atrevida: 4, 7, 36, 66,
    67, 73, 76, 79, 80, 86, 89, 91, 103,
    108, 112, 117, 129, 158, 163, 165
Domínguez, Father Francisco: 46

Echeagaray, Manuel de: 37
Echeverría, Atanasio: 73, 93, 94
Elisa, Francisco: 165
Espinosa y Tello, Josef: 22, 23, 97,
    97 n, 164 n
Esselen (Eslen) Indians: 12, 13, 82, 87,
    89, 113, 132, 139, 142–45; vo-
    cabulary of, 147–49; catechism of,
    151–55; see also Rumsen Indians
Expedition of the Limits to the North of
    California (1792): 73, 93

Fages, Pedro: 32, 33, 35, 36, 44,
    121 n; exploration by, 45–46
Fernando VII: 52, 53, 58, 77, 78
Ferrer Maldonado, Strait of: 4
Fidalgo, Salvador: 111, 111 n
Fuca, Strait of Juan de (Entrada de
    Fuca): 3, 4, 22, 23, 57, 72, 76, 103,
    104, 106, 113, 162

Galleons: 44, 63, 97, 114, 114 n, 128
Garcés, Father Francisco: 46
Gertrudis (Santa Gertrudis) (naval vessel):
    17, 87, 89, 91–93, 109, 146, 158,
    167

Godoy, Manuel: 76
Gray, Robert: 93, 106, 107
Guest, Father Francis: 11–12
Gutiérrez de la Concha, Juan: 62

Haenke, Tadeo: 117, 117 n
Hawaii: 43
Hezeta, Bruno de: 103 n, 107
Hezeta Entrance (Entrada de Hezeta),
    15, 103, 106, 108, 109

Indian activities: 134, 140, 142,
    144–46
Isabela Island: 98, 99, 165, 167
Iturbide, Agustín: 85

Kenneally, Father Finbar: 12

Lángara, Juan de: 63
Langsdorff, Georg von: 13, 14
La Pérouse, Count of: 12, 13, 35, 47,
    121 n, 129, 137
Lasuén, Father Fermín Francisco de: 9,
    12, 17, 29, 30, 47, 82, 94, 129,
    130 n, 134, 146; report on status of
    missions, 33; biography, 85–87; aid
    to visitors, 88–89; vocabulary of In-
    dians, 147–49; catechism, 151–55
Los Angeles pueblo: 28, 30, 34

Malaspina, Alejandro: 4, 5, 10 ff; expe-
    dition of, 11, 21, 30, 42, 47, 62,
    82; opinion of Lasuén, 12, 86; in-
    quiries by, 32, 33; opinion on fur
    trade, 44; assistance given, 86; opin-
    ion of Pedro Ramos, 80; correspon-
    dence with Lasuén, 88–89
Malvinas Islands: 55
Manzanelli, Nicolás: 44
Marías Islands, 98, 99, 150, 165–67
Marquina, Joaquin: 97, 98
Martínez, Estevan José: 44
Matute, Juan: 162, 162 n
Mendocino, Cape: 3, 103, 108
Mesa, Father José María de: 66
Mexicana (schooner) (María Santísima de

la Asunción): see *Sutil* and *Mexicana*
Mexico: 11 ff; Mexico City, 12, 17, 25 ff
Mission activity: 128–32, 136–38; criticism of, 138–39; status report, 160
Monterey: 4, 13 ff; capital of California, 28, 31, 68; presidio of, 34, 35, 41, 82, 84; port of, 50, 80, 103, 108, 109, 113, 114; Indians of, 132
Monterrey, Count of: 119, 119 n
Mourelle, Francisco Antonio: 5, 37–40, 42, 45, 46
Moziño, José Mariano: 88, 93, 94, 119
Mulgrave, Port of (Alaska): 68, 74

Navarrete, Martín Fernández de: 23
Nelson, Horatio: 59
New Mexico (Spanish province): 40, 46
Nootka, Santa Cruz de: 3, 4, 14, 27 ff; Nootka Sound Controversy, 30, 42, 71
Novo y Colson, Pedro de: 20
Núñez Gaona, Port of: 109, 109 n, 113

Pantheon of Illustrious Mariners, near Cádiz: 40, 53
Pantoja, Juan: 47
Parma, Duchy of: 20
Pelayo (Spanish warship): 77
Pérez Hernández, Juan José: 36, 94
Pérez de Tagle, José: 44
Philippines: 7, 39, 62, 63; ship, 114, 128
Princesa (frigate): 111, 111 n, 112

Quimper, Manuel: 167, 167 n

Ramos, Pedro: 79–80
Ravenet, Juan: 68
Realejo, Port of (Nicaragua): 67
Revilla Gigedo, Count of: 5, 7, 19, 23, 38, 57, 67, 81
Rezanof, Nicolai: 47, 84
Roméu, José Antonio: 33, 35–37, 41; widow of, 92, 94
Rumsen (Runsien) Indians: 12, 13, 82, 87, 89, 113, 132, 139, 142–45;

vocabulary of, 147–49; catechism of, 151–55; see also Esselen Indians

Sacramento, Colonia de (Uruguay): 55, 74
Saint Helens, Mount: 14, 15, 17 n, 104
Sal, Hermenegildo: 30, 94, 121 n
Salamanca, Secundino: 7, 21, 25, 61, 62, 94; biography, 63–64
San Blas (Mexican port): 14, 44 ff; naval department of, 5, 6, 8, 17, 27, 39, 89, 114, 136, 165; vessels of, 82; pilots' map, 95, 158, 163
San Buenaventura (mission): 85
San Carlos (mission): 12, 13, 31, 82, 84–87, 113, 117, 145, 146; see also Carmelo
San Diego: 97, 150, 161–63, 165; presidio of, 28, 34; mission of, 29
San Fernando de México, College of: 12, 31, 85, 87, 129, 138
San Francisco: presidio of, 28, 34, 84; mission of, 29, 47; Farallones of, 108
San Fulgencio (Spanish warship): 51, 58, 66, 71, 76
San Gabriel (mission): 35, 84
San Isidro (Spanish vessel): 57
San Joaquin Valley: 45, 46
San José (pueblo): 28, 30, 34
San Juan Capistrano (mission): 35
San Lucas, Cape: 150, 163, 165
San Pedro Alcántara (Spanish vessel): 25, 58
Santa Barbara: presidio, 28, 84; channel, 88, 150, 158; island, 161
Santa Catalina Island: 143, 161, 162
Santa Clara (mission): 117
Santa Cruz (mission): 29–31, 38
Señán, Father José Francisco de Paula: 82, 94, 129 n; biography, 85
Serra, Father Junípero: 29, 85–87
Servin, Manuel: 37
Soledad, La (mission): 29–31
Sonora (Spanish vessel): 5, 90, 105, 105 n
Suría, Tomás de: 13, 67, 68

Sutil and *Mexicana* (schooners): 3, 4 ff;
  exploration of Channel Islands,
  95–97; search for Los Alijos, 98,
  150, 164; journal of 1792 voyage,
  103–67

Tofiño, Vicente: 50, 56, 61, 63
Torres-Guerra, Alonso: 87–90, 94,
  109, 146; biography, 91–92
Trafalgar, Battle of: 21, 51, 59, 64,
  162 n

Valdés, Cayetano: 3, 5 ff; biography,
  49–53
Valdés y Bazán, Antonio: 49, 72
Vancouver, George: 12, 13, 30, 47,
  90, 93, 103, 106, 112, 112 n
Vancouver Island: 3, 27, 68; circum-
navigation of, 19, 38, 69, 71, 81, 95
Vargas Ponce, José: 10–11
Vasadre y Vega, Vicente: 44
Vélez de Escalante, Father Silvestre: 46
Vencedor (Spanish warship): 58
Venegas, Father Miguel: 9, 132 ff
Veracruz (Mexican port): 25, 50, 58,
  70, 93, 99
Vernacci, Juan: 7, 19, 21, 25, 26, 57,
  75, 94; biography, 61–63
Vizcaíno, Sebastián: 119, 119 n, 120 n,
  132, 143, 163, 163 n

Weatherhead, Matthew: 92–94, 119 n

Yakutat Bay: 68, 74

Zócalo, Mexico City: 70, 73, 74